A Guide to Useful Evaluation of Language Programs

Related Works from Georgetown University Press

Useful Assessment and Evaluation in Language Education
JOHN McE. DAVIS, JOHN M. NORRIS, MARGARET E. MALONE, TODD H. McKAY, and YOUNG-A SON, EDITORS

To Advanced Proficiency and Beyond: Theory and Methods for Developing Superior Second Language Ability
TONY BROWN and JENNIFER BOWN, EDITORS

Innovative Strategies for Heritage Language Teaching: A Practical Guide for the Classroom
MARTA FAIRCLOUGH and SARA M. BEAUDRIE, EDITORS, FOREWORD by ANA ROCA, AFTERWORD by GUADALUPE VALDÉS

A GUIDE TO USEFUL EVALUATION
OF LANGUAGE PROGRAMS

John McE. Davis and Todd H. McKay, Editors

Assessment and Evaluation
Language Resource Center

GEORGETOWN UNIVERSITY PRESS
Washington, DC

The publisher is not responsible for third-party websites or their content. URL links were active at time of publication.

Library of Congress Cataloging-in-Publication Data

Names: Davis, John McE., 1970- editor. | McKay, Todd H., editor.
Title: A Guide to Useful Evaluation of Language Programs / John McE. Davis
   and Todd H. McKay, editors.
Description: Washington, DC : Georgetown University Press, 2018. | Includes
   bibliographical references and index.
Identifiers: LCCN 2017036651 | ISBN 9781626165762 (hardcover : alk. paper) |
ISBN 9781626165779 (pb : alk. paper) | ISBN 9781626165786 (eb)
Subjects: LCSH: Language and languages–Study and teaching–Evaluation.
Classification: LCC P53.63 .G85 2018 | DDC 418.0071–dc23
LC record available at https://lccn.loc.gov/2017036651

19 18   9 8 7 6 5 4 3 2   First printing

Printed in the United States of America

Contents

Illustrations

Figures

Tables

Preface

THIS VOLUME PROVIDES LANGUAGE educators with strategies and techniques for evaluating language education programs. It issues out of support and training initiatives offered by the Assessment and Evaluation Language Resource Center (AELRC), a Title VI–funded research and training entity dedicated to facilitating useful assessment and evaluation practices that help foreign language (FL) educators innovate and improve their programs, ensure accountability to students and society, and articulate and express the value of FL studies in the world today.[1] More specifically, this book originated in an AERLC-sponsored workshop at the 2016 Georgetown University Round Table (GURT) on Languages and Linguistics, entitled Useful Evaluation in Language Programs. The workshop was also the product of an ongoing AELRC research agenda investigating how evaluation and assessment can be best implemented in language programs as mechanisms for improving language teaching and learning. The AELRC workshop, then, aimed to train educators in a specific approach to evaluation that focuses on concretely using evaluation for inquiry, evidence-based practice, and organizational learning. We carry on this conceptualization here, advancing the notion that evaluation can be a powerful driver of positive change with the potential to do considerable good in language education programs.

A number of individuals and entities have made this book possible. First, I would like to express my appreciation and gratitude to my coauthor and coeditor, Todd McKay, for his essential contributions. Todd has a long history with the AELRC and deep involvement in various program evaluation and assessment initiatives at Georgetown and beyond. His considerable knowledge and research expertise were an invaluable resource, as was his tireless labor and good humor. It was truly a pleasure to work with him.

I also want to sincerely thank the contributors, Lara Bryfonski, Amy Kim, Jorge Méndez Seijas, Francesca Venezia, Cristi Vallejos, and Janire Zalbidea, graduate students at Georgetown University and alumni of the Department of Linguistics course on language program evaluation. Each has gone on to develop evaluation skills and research specializations in interesting and novel directions, and the book has benefited greatly from their expertise, hard work, and high-quality contributions.

My thanks also to AELRC director Margaret Malone, as always, for supporting and encouraging the project from its inception at GURT 2016 through to the realization of this work. Finally, we are especially indebted to Hope LeGro at Georgetown University Press for her initial interest in the GURT workshop for publication and Glenn Saltzman for her support and assistance throughout the publishing process.

The individuals involved in the creation of this work have aimed to provide language educators with a helpful resource for using evaluation to better understand and improve language education. It is my sincere hope that readers will be empowered by this guide to do useful evaluation that does good for themselves, their students, their colleagues, and their communities.

—John McE. Davis
Centreville, Virginia

Note

1. AELRC is sponsored by a grant from the US Department of Education (P229A140012).

1

An Introduction to Useful and Used Evaluation in Language Education

JOHN McE. DAVIS

THE GOAL OF THIS book is to help language educators conduct useful evaluation in language education programs. It comes at a time in language education when instructors are increasingly called upon to conduct evaluation themselves in their classrooms and institutions. Growing desires for educational accountability and quality assurance have led to increased evaluation and assessment requirements imposed by accreditors, school districts, and federal and state governments (to name a few). While contemporary evaluation in language education is still often conducted by peer reviewers and evaluation professionals (as has been the practice for many years), more and more commonly the responsibility for doing evaluation now falls to the language instructor, lead teacher, section chair, or curriculum committee. The primary aim of this book, then, is to help language educators meet the various contemporary demands for evaluation and assessment now commonplace in US language education, and to conduct evaluation in ways that lead to meaningful programmatic decisions and change.

In addition, this guide advocates for a particular view of evaluation as an inherently worthwhile mode of educational inquiry, rather than merely a process of judging educational quality. We further suggest that evaluation is most effective when its impetus is less a reaction to outside requirements and more something that emanates naturally and organically from within a program where instructors, administrators, and leadership take ownership of evaluation and engage in consistent, evidence-based decision-making. In the same way that time, effort, and resources are routinely dedicated to teaching, curriculum review, assessment, and professional development, so too should evaluation be an integral part of the daily business of teaching languages. To these ends, our aim is to impart foundational evaluation knowledge and skills that help create a "culture of evaluation" and enable stakeholders to better understand and improve language teaching and learning.

Evaluation Use and Usefulness

Conducting useful evaluation is a deceptively straightforward aim. Doing evaluation that results in concrete action, decision-making, and meaningful change is, in fact, a tremendous challenge. An important goal for this book, then, is to help readers plan and implement evaluation in a way that enhances the ultimate usefulness and use of evaluation in language programs.

This may seem like a banal and obvious point. Of course evaluation should be useful. Why make this distinction? Naturally, educators and other stakeholders need information to better understand and improve their programs, and evaluation is a process that helps them do this. By its very nature, evaluation is a useful activity. Why state the obvious?

In fact, research has shown, to the contrary, that evaluation is vulnerable to non-usefulness and lacking use of evaluation findings. Despite a considerable potential for shedding light on issues and problems in educational programs, evaluation does not always straightforwardly lead to this end. Indeed, readers may have experienced instances where evaluation activities failed to have intended or useful impacts. Perhaps recommendations from a program review failed to be implemented. Perhaps student and teacher evaluations are collected consistently but without any demonstrable use toward improvement or change. Perhaps requirements from the university or college administration to engage in assessment of student outcomes has created additional work and taken up valuable time but without any tangible benefits to student learning or teaching.

If these scenarios sound familiar, they are examples of a lesson long learned in evaluation research and practice—the efficacy and usefulness of an evaluation is not a given. Rather, actual use of evaluation findings is something evaluators must carefully plan for and nurture throughout an evaluation project (Norris 2016). This being the case, we advocate in this book for an evaluation approach that calls for an intentional and systematic focus on evaluation use and usefulness throughout evaluation planning and implementation. It is an approach strongly influenced by the ideas of Michael Quinn Patton and his "utilization-focused" evaluation model, and also elaborated by the main proponent of a use-focused evaluation approach in language education, John Norris (2006, 2008, 2016).

Patton (2008, 37) defines utilization-focused evaluation as follows:

> Utilization-focused evaluation is evaluation done for and with specific intended primary users for specific, intended uses. Utilization-focused evaluation begins with the premise that evaluations should be judged by their utility and actual use; therefore, evaluators should facilitate the evaluation process and design any evaluation with careful consideration for how everything that is done, from beginning to end, will affect use. Use concerns how real people in the real world apply evaluation findings and experience the evaluation process. Therefore, the focus in utilization-focused evaluation is on intended use by intended users.

"Careful consideration for how everything ... will affect use" calls for specific evaluation planning and implementation techniques. Adding to the traditionally technical aspects of evaluation such as data collection, analysis, or reporting, a use-focused evaluation approach integrates specific strategies into the evaluation process that help increase the likelihood that evaluation findings actually get used. To give a brief example of what this entails, in a use-focused evaluation approach, the evaluator does not conduct an evaluation assuming that program leadership will use the evaluation results and implement the evaluator's findings. Instead, the evaluator identifies and engages *specific users of the evaluation* during evaluation planning and designs the evaluation carefully to meet those individuals' needs. In addition, the evaluator does not assume or guess what decision-makers will do with the evaluation findings once the evaluation report has been submitted. Rather, a use-focused approach calls for the evaluator to sit down with decision-makers and list out in explicit terms specifically *what they want to do* with evaluation results. The evaluator then organizes the subsequent evaluation steps and phases in specific ways so that the project supplies decision-makers with the findings they need in order to do what they need to do in their programs.

These and other use-focused strategies are key elements of a use-focused evaluation approach. They are intended to help ensure that when the evaluation results are presented in the final report or presentation, specific intended users will actually use the information from the evaluation for specific intended uses. We propose that language education would profit from integrating an explicitly use-focused evaluation approach into current evaluation activities in language programs (along with Norris 2006, 2008, 2016). A methodological focus on usefulness is now an established part of evaluation outside of language education and an essential aspect of professional evaluation practice, as formalized in the JCSEE[1] *Program Evaluation Standards* (Yarbrough et al. 2011). The JCSEE evaluation standards lay out expectations of high-quality evaluation for professional evaluators, one of which emphasizes "utility" and ensuring that the evaluation is useful for—and used by—program stakeholders. Furthermore, the factors that lead to evaluation usefulness have been a focal concern of program evaluation research, a key finding of which is that intentionally planning for evaluation usefulness leads to evaluation use. Lastly, a number of recent evaluation case studies in language programs have showcased use-focused techniques and productively useful program development outcomes as a result of adopting this approach (see Norris and Davis 2015; Norris et al. 2009). A use-focused approach to evaluation, then, has much to recommend and offers considerable potential for language educators to better understand and improve language instruction.

Evaluation

We define evaluation in this book using a definition from Norris (2006, 579), which highlights key aspects of the evaluation process we aim to emphasize:

> Evaluation is the gathering of information about any of the variety of elements that constitute educational programs, for a variety of purposes that include primarily understanding, demonstrating, improving, and judging program value. . .

Following Norris, evaluation in our view is more than judging program value or effectiveness, though this is certainly an important evaluation purpose, as Norris has captured here. Rather, we envision evaluation more generally as a mode of inquiry in which stakeholders within language programs collect, learn from, and use evidence toward programmatic actions and decisions. In addition, we echo Norris' (2006) observation that the link between gathering information and using that information is a tenuous one. It is precisely this link in the sequence of events of an evaluation project that this guide attempts to strengthen, and we offer the use-focused evaluation approach as a strategy to do so.

Intended Audience

This volume is intended to be a practical manual that language educators and administrators can use to implement evaluation in ways that enhance methodological quality and lead to useful actions and decisions. It is not aimed at professional evaluators, academics, or evaluation consultants. Rather, the intended audience is readers with little or no evaluation experience who need straightforward, practical guidance on how to plan an evaluation, collect useful information on a programmatic issue of interest, and enable stakeholders to make programmatic decisions on the basis of evidence. To that end, this book is meant to be a step-by-step guide for evaluation novices within language educational institutions who are responsible for evaluation activities. Again, such responsibilities now commonly and increasingly issue from external mandates and create a burden of labor for language professionals who typically lack the resources and expertise to meet those demands successfully.

Organization of the Volume

The book is organized according to the chronological steps for planning an evaluation project, laying out the key considerations and strategies needed to plan and conduct evaluation in a language education program.

Chapter 2 (Best Practices for Evaluation Success) explains how useful evaluation relies heavily on specific program conditions, infrastructures, and personnel dimensions, each of which should (optimally) be present in programs before evaluation begins. The chapter emphasizes that evaluation can succeed or fail depending on the conduciveness of the programmatic context to high-quality evaluation activities.

Chapter 3 (Planning for Useful Evaluation: Users, Uses, Questions) describes the essential aspects of use-focused evaluation planning. Specifically, the chapter emphasizes two cornerstone planning components of Patton's framework: the identification of (1) evaluation users and (2) evaluation uses. In addition, the chapter describes how to develop evaluation questions so that an evaluation project proceeds systematically with clear aims.

Chapter 4 (Identifying Indicators) provides advice on identifying and developing "indicators" of language program functionality—that is, the educational processes or phenomena within the program that will be captured or measured during the evaluation project. Chapter 4 stresses the importance of identifying program indicators before selecting data-collection methods and discusses the threats to evaluation usefulness when failing to think first about the *types of information* needed to answer evaluation questions.

Chapter 5 (Selecting Methods, Collecting Data) introduces the range of evaluation data-collection methods available to language educators. Chapter 5 also discusses issues that impact the usefulness of evaluation information and proposes strategies for choosing methods that help ensure the information will be what users and stakeholders want and need.

Chapters 6, 7, and 8 provide more detailed methodological advice on the three most common tools or strategies for collecting evaluation information: focus groups, interviews, and questionnaires (with the exception of language assessment). Each chapter discusses

(1) the evaluation-related purpose of the method; (2) the unique advantages (and pitfalls) of a particular method; (3) the main steps in planning, designing, and administering the data-collection method; and (4) best practices for implementing each technique.

Chapter 9 (Analyzing Evaluation Data) provides introductory advice on analyzing the likely data coming from questionnaires and focus groups. In addition, key considerations of data trustworthiness are discussed as they pertain to evaluation projects.

Chapter 10 (Key Points to Remember for Useful Evaluation) summarizes the most important points from the guide, providing a list of priority evaluation best practices.

Chapter 11 (Example Evaluation Plan) provides an example evaluation plan so that readers can understand what an evaluation plan looks like and how the various use-focused evaluation components come together, including a description of the program background, stakeholder engagement plan, project users, uses, evaluation questions, indicators, data-collection tools, and project timeline.

Evaluation Scenarios

To help illustrate the concepts presented in this guide, three fictional evaluation scenarios are provided and elaborated in subsequent chapters as example cases of how to plan and implement use-focused evaluation techniques. The scenarios are developed throughout the book to help readers better understand evaluation concepts from a given chapter. For example, at the end of chapter 3, fictional evaluation users, uses, and questions are provided for each scenario so that readers can see what these specific elements of evaluation planning might look like. The three scenarios are (1) a community college language lab, (2) a language program needs analysis for adult learners, and (3) a high school Chinese telecollaboration program. Each scenario is described in detail below.

Scenario 1: Community College Language Lab

A group of language instructors at a city community college is responsible for managing a language media center. The chair of the humanities division is concerned with the lab's effectiveness. She is interested in making the lab support student learning more effectively. The chair asks the instructors to conduct an evaluation to investigate how useful the lab is for various campus stakeholders. The lab is located in one large classroom and has desktop computers with headsets and a large digital projector. The lab staff consists of one paid coordinator and two student volunteers. The students who use the lab are from diverse cultural and educational backgrounds; many are heritage language learners.

Scenario 2: Adult Language Program Needs Analysis

A group of teachers provides language instruction for adult learners at a small, state government-funded English language program. The students are recent immigrants from Latin American countries who need basic English skills for living and working in the United States. The director of the program has asked for an evaluation since it has become unclear whether the current curriculum (unchanged for many years) meets the practical language needs of students to live and work in their communities. Students enter the program with varying levels of education and come from diverse professional backgrounds in their home countries. Ages range from early twenties to late fifties.

Scenario 3: Chinese Telecollaboration

A group of high school Chinese language teachers and a selection of eleventh-grade students have been participating in a telecollaboration program with a partner Chinese secondary school (where Chinese students are learning English). The principal of the US-based school has called for an evaluation of the impact of the telecollaboration program on student learning and has delegated that responsibility to the school language teachers. The principal and other school administrators are interested in determining whether the program should be expanded to all eleventh-grade classes. Currently, twenty participating students meet twice a week for an hour with their language partners and communicate via Skype. The program is sixteen weeks long. The teachers use a "shared text" method where students read the same text translated into Chinese and English beforehand and then discuss the text when they chat via Skype. The telecollaboration sessions happen in the library using school computers.

As readers work through the guide, each of these scenarios appears throughout the various chapters along with fictional examples of how the various evaluation steps discussed in this book might be designed and implemented. For example, in the next chapter, we explain how to plan an evaluation project in a specific way so that it provides useful information that actually gets used to do something concretely productive in a language program. Namely, we discuss how stakeholders and key evaluation users should be identified and consulted early in project planning so that the evaluation results and findings will be what stakeholders want and need for important program decision-making. To demonstrate these key concepts from the chapter, we provide examples of likely stakeholders and evaluation users for each of the example scenarios. In a similar way, we continue to develop the scenarios throughout the guide, showing concrete examples of evaluation strategies in each of the following chapters.

Note

1.   JCSEE stands for Joint Committee on Standards for Educational Evaluation.

2

Best Practices for Language Program Evaluation Success

JOHN McE. DAVIS

BEFORE DISCUSSING THE SPECIFIC steps in planning and conducting an evaluation project using a use-focused approach, this chapter explains some general evaluation best practices and key concepts that will enable educators to conduct productively useful evaluation in their language programs. For example, useful evaluation depends on how well the evaluation is conducted. Thus, in chapters 3–8, we lay out specific evaluation planning and implementation strategies that help ensure evaluation quality, advocating, again, for a specifically use-focused evaluation approach.

In this chapter, however, we discuss key aspects of program context, personnel factors, and other general implementation concerns that will help evaluation be a successful endeavor. Recall Norris' (2006, 579) definition of evaluation from chapter 1: "Evaluation is the gathering of information about any of the variety of elements that constitute educational programs, for a variety of purposes that include primarily understanding, demonstrating, improving, and judging program value." As suggested in Norris' definition, evaluation can be a powerful tool for developing, improving, understanding, or demonstrating the value of language teaching and learning. When conducted well and in a set of conducive programmatic conditions, evaluation is powerful force for positive change. For example, evaluation can aid staff and other stakeholders in learning about how well their program is functioning. Evaluation can help programs know whether students are reaching important learning targets and whether important institutional goals are being met. Evaluation enables administrators and leadership to conduct strategic planning, make important decisions on the basis of evidence, meet external accountability requirements, or justify requests for resources and funding. Evaluation can also engage program stakeholders and promote commitment to institutional objectives. Evaluation can also help programs demonstrate their worth and importance to the local community, or even the value of language education, generally, for an educated society and literate citizenry.

Using evaluation productively toward these estimable aims, however, depends on a number of factors. As noted in chapter 1, evaluation does not naturally lead to these ends. On the one hand, evaluation activities must be conducted at a high level of quality. This means the evaluation project must be planned and implemented systematically with involvement and buy-in from relevant stakeholders. Also, the evaluation must produce information that is clear, nonthreatening, timely, sufficiently trustworthy, and perceived as issuing from sound data-collection methods. And perhaps most importantly, the productive use of an evaluation will strongly depend on sustained stakeholder involvement and participation.

Other factors that will impact the efficacy of the evaluation will have more to do with the evaluation context. For example, the information needs of decision-makers, the political climate, competing information from other sources, the general commitment or receptiveness to evaluation within the program, and stakeholder engagement during the evaluation process; all of these more local concerns will affect how impactful an evaluation will be (Johnson et al. 2009). The aim of this chapter is to describe some of the more general contextual, personnel-related, and methodological factors that help evaluation to be a useful activity—ideas that should be kept in mind when getting started with evaluation for the first time.

A Case Study of Useful Evaluation

Before proceeding further, readers might reflect for a moment on how productive evaluation activities are in their programs currently. Is there consistent and productive use of evaluation information? If not, why might this be the case? What is preventing evaluation from supplying people with the information they need to improve instruction or make other important educational decisions? Is evaluation something that people value in the same way as curriculum design, materials development, teacher training, or language assessment? If not, why not? To help explore some of these issues as well as illustrate some of the factors that help evaluation succeed, we present the following real-life evaluation example from a language program with a long history of useful evaluation and evidence-based practice, and we highlight what educators did in this brief case study that made evaluation successful.

Case Study Program Context
A university French department has been conducting evaluation and improvement-oriented assessment for many years. The current chair of the program is committed to using evaluation for improving teaching and learning in the program. A former chair and respected senior faculty member is a well-known researcher on language pedagogy and assessment and has spearheaded evaluation efforts in the program for many years. Evaluation and assessment are integral parts of the department's administrative processes. Programmatic decisions are often made on the basis of evaluation evidence. In addition, the program consistently tries to improve and enhance the evaluation knowledge and skills of faculty and staff, bringing in experts to conduct workshops and to help facilitate evaluation projects. Lastly, new hires into the program are expected to have evaluation and assessment knowledge.

Project Impetus

The chair has successfully secured extra funding from the university administration for a new evaluation project. Findings and lessons learned from past evaluation projects have led to the creation of an innovative French writing curriculum, and the faculty and chair want to better understand how well the curriculum is functioning in first-year courses.

Project Planning

In the very early planning stages, careful consideration is given to the stakeholders of the evaluation. A wide range of program stakeholders (including students) are consulted for their views on what and how to evaluate courses at the first-year level. The specific users of the evaluation are identified as well as their intended uses of the evaluation results (see chapter 3). Additional advice is provided by a leading evaluation expert brought in to help with planning and to conduct workshops on assessment and data collection. Evaluation stakeholders are kept informed on the progress of the evaluation via occasional emails and social media notifications. Students, instructors, and faculty are involved in data collection. The project is conducted quickly and efficiently. Stakeholders are provided opportunities to help analyze and interpret data.

Reporting

A written evaluation report is circulated via email throughout the department and posted on the department website (requiring a login). Results are shared at a department meeting with students and other stakeholders in attendance. A plan and timeline are created for using results and implementing recommendations.

Project Uses

Findings are used in a variety of productive ways. A number of changes are made to the curriculum, materials, and assessments. The results from the evaluation are used to make a request to the university administration for extra funding. The project is used for the annual institutional review report to the administration. The evaluation process is used intentionally to increase involvement of graduate students in educational innovation and program development. Two of the faculty publish on the project, and the paper is used as part of one faculty member's tenure review.

Evaluation Best Practices

What made this evaluation successful? What led to the various concretely productive uses of the project by different program stakeholders? We use this example to identify and highlight a number of specific evaluation practices and strategies that are known to increase evaluation impact and effectiveness. We suggest that these are key concepts and practices to keep in mind at various stages of an evaluation project. The factors demonstrated in the French program example that led to useful evaluation include (1) stakeholder involvement, (2) stakeholder learning, (3) shared understanding of evaluation, (4) effective communication, (5) feasibility, (6) high-quality practices, (7) strong evaluation knowledge and skills, (8) ample evaluation resources, (9) effective program leadership, and (10) evaluation ownership.

Stakeholder Involvement

Perhaps the single most important insight gained from evaluation research is that stakeholder involvement in all aspects and at all stages of an evaluation is crucially important to evaluation success.

Recall in the French program example that evaluators actively involved stakeholders throughout the evaluation project. Program stakeholders—including students—were involved in data collection, analysis, and interpretation. We explore this topic in greater detail in chapter 3, but for now, it is important to note that the usefulness and productiveness of evaluation is greatly increased when it proceeds democratically, with everyone "on board," and when it reflects and responds to stakeholders' interests. A number of key implications for how to do evaluation issue from this insight. During initial discussions, for example, when evaluation is being planned, it is necessary to include as many relevant stakeholders (or stakeholder group representatives) from the program as possible and practicable. To this end, there are a few key groups to target. People in leadership roles are especially important since these individuals will be instrumental in supporting evaluation efforts and using evaluation results in decision-making. Also note in the French program example that students were included in evaluation activities. Students bring a useful perspective to evaluation efforts. They can speak to evaluation needs and respond well to involvement in educational decision-making that ultimately impacts them most. More detailed advice for organizing stakeholder involvement is provided in chapter 3, but we introduce here the important idea that to maximize evaluation usefulness, stakeholders must be actively engaged and involved in the evaluation project from start to finish.

Stakeholder Learning

Another important benefit from stakeholder participation should also be noted: When stakeholders participate in evaluation, they deepen their understanding of the educational processes happening within their program. Evaluation participants, then, learn as much about their programs from being *involved in evaluation processes* as they do from the evaluation findings and final report. While readers may assume that the evaluation report findings are what increases people's knowledge (which is mostly correct), evaluation participation itself is, in fact, equally enlightening. As we describe later in the book, engaging stakeholders in evaluation planning, having them help collect and analyze data, and providing opportunities for collaborative interpretation of results (among other activities) all help stakeholders to better understand what is happening in the program, how the program functions, and what can be changed or improved on the basis of evidence. Evaluation participation also teaches stakeholders how to do evaluation, which improves the quality of evaluation efforts and gets people in the habit of systematic inquiry and making decisions on the basis of evidence. These various benefits, then, are important to take advantage of so that evaluation has a meaningful impact on as many people in the program as possible.

Shared Understandings

How people within a program think and feel about evaluation will impact its effectiveness. For evaluation to be useful, stakeholders will need to think about evaluation in similar ways and will need to have a shared understanding of why evaluation is happening. The purpose of an evaluation project, then, will need to be clear to key stakeholders (see chapter 3) and communicated early so that everyone has the same project expectations.

In addition, evaluation proceeds best when people are generally accepting of the process and think evaluation is a useful and viable tool for improving teaching and learning. Naturally, readers undertaking evaluation in their programs may be limited in their ability to influence the attitudes and thinking of others. In such cases, it may be best to involve willing and enthusiastic stakeholder participants initially in evaluation efforts and politely exclude unsupportive individuals who may hinder evaluation efforts. Evaluation can be a threatening concept, and an evaluation project—particularly one that lacks transparency—may generate suspicion and other negative attitudes that can thwart an evaluation project before it has even begun. However, fears can be allayed by involving stakeholders in evaluation activities and communicating clearly throughout the evaluation project, a topic we discuss next.

Communication

In the French program example, intentional steps were taken to communicate about the evaluation project to program stakeholders in various ways. Email, social media, meetings, and the department website were used to circulate information about all aspects and stages of the evaluation. Effective communication and related outreach efforts help considerably with stakeholder engagement and participation. At the minimum, effective communication means that evaluation findings are shared widely with relevant stakeholders using a variety of outlets (shared report, public presentation, social media, publication, etc.) and that findings are reported in a clear, relevant, meaningful, and nonthreatening way. Beyond reporting on findings, information about evaluation activities, plans, and happenings should be shared with relevant stakeholders frequently and using technology and other methods so that evaluation information is easy to find (e.g., email lists, a program website, social media). Finally, systematic record-keeping of evaluation activities (e.g., collection of reports, plans, meeting minutes) helps to keep track of the evaluation history of the program and preserves institutional memory of evaluation work for future projects.

Feasibility

One of the key insights into making evaluation useful is that evaluators should only start evaluations that have a reasonable chance of actually getting done. Projects that are too ambitious in scope risk either failing to conclude or investigating a program element superficially. All things being equal, if evaluation is happening in the program for the first time, we tentatively recommend a small, circumscribed evaluation project to get things started (if possible). A modest project has a number of attractive aspects. First, a useful assessment project is necessarily a finished one, and a small, feasible project may be easier to accomplish in a timely way. Further, a smaller project will likely require less in the way of resources, which will be helpful if such resources are unavailable or scarce. Also, a modest, initial evaluation success over the short term will demonstrate the usefulness and efficacy of evaluation to leadership and other program stakeholders, potentially generate support for future projects, and possibly win over those who lacked enthusiasm the first time around. Ultimately, of course, the size and scope of an assessment or evaluation project will be determined by the particular needs and purposes of local stakeholders. The above advice, then, is simply to point out that when considering an evaluation project, feasibility and the likelihood of really getting a project done should be kept in mind.

High-Quality Practices

The French program demonstrated a number of evaluation implementation best practices that helped make the project a success. Primary among them was the way in which evaluation users and uses were all listed in explicit terms, these steps being key features of a use-focused evaluation approach. We discuss these strategies in detail in chapter 3 and the remainder of the book, but it is worth noting early that a use-focused approach was a key factor in making the French evaluation a success.

In addition to use-focused methods, the French example demonstrates a number of other evaluation best practices. For example, this project was not a one-off; evaluation had been happening cyclically for many years prior, building on findings from previous cycles of evaluation. As a result, individuals in the program had considerable evaluation experience and thus a certain amount of evaluation skill and expertise (see next section). In addition, the project was conducted quickly and efficiently, and a plan and timeline were generated for using results, creating a clear road map for evaluation use. And since the project was conducted quickly, the results were timely and available for program decision-making. Furthermore, the information provided by the evaluation was accurate and regarded as trustworthy by decision-makers.

In addition to these exemplary practices in the French program case-study, evaluators should also strive for data-collection and analysis methods that are comprehensible, and—on the face of things—trustworthy to users and stakeholders. Also, both quantitative (numerical or statistical) and qualitative (textual or written) information should be collected to shed light on evaluation queries from different perspectives and using different types of evidence (see chapter 5). And finally, the evaluation process must be seen by users and stakeholders as unbiased and conducted by evaluators who are trustworthy and credible.

Evaluation Knowledge and Skills

High-quality evaluation practices usually are the result of strong evaluation knowledge and skills, as evidenced in the French program example. The primary purpose of this book is to help language educators develop such skills by providing key concepts and techniques for implementing useful evaluation in language programs. To the extent possible, then, it is important for anyone new to evaluation to self-educate, read evaluation and assessment literature, and participate in available workshops and hands-on training opportunities. To these ends, we particularly recommend looking into resources and training offered by the Assessment and Evaluation Language Resource Center (AELRC).[1] AELRC resources are specifically designed for language program evaluation and language educators (and funded by the federal government for this purpose). Another set of useful resources is provided by the Foreign Language Program Evaluation Project,[2] an initiative of the National Foreign Language Resource Center (NFLRC). Both entities offer how-to information, workshops, conferences, and notifications on evaluation–related happenings in language education. Both websites also showcase numerous research projects receiving AELRC/ NFLRC support and assistance. A notable example from the AELRC is an annotated bibliography of evaluation-related studies capturing K–16 educators' experiences using evaluation toward program development and other educational uses. These useful examples demonstrate the possibilities for understanding and innovating language programs using evaluation methods.

Resources

Like any dedicated educational activity, evaluation is more effective when there are sufficient supporting resources. Note that the French program enjoyed a number of resources to help their evaluation efforts. Most notably, extra funding had been secured for the project. Funding for evaluation helps in a number of important ways. It can be used to purchase needed equipment (e.g., recording devices for interviews), software, and reference materials or to bring in assessment experts or consultants (as in the French program example). In addition, evaluation often requires a certain amount of labor—to collect and analyze data in particular—and funding can be used to recruit personnel via course buyouts or to pay graduate or teaching assistants for evaluation work. Over the longer term, funds can be used for evaluation professional development, such as attending evaluation-related conferences or workshops, or to purchase professional memberships. All of the above expenditures either create the time needed to conduct evaluation successfully or enhance the evaluation knowledge and skills of individuals doing the evaluation, both elements important for evaluation usefulness.

Of course, US K–16 education is routinely short on funding, but with some persistent searching, readers may find that evaluation funding is available. Many larger educational institutions will provide dedicated evaluation funding and we have seen educators unaware that such resources exist. Entreaties should also be made to department or program leadership since these individuals are increasingly open and willing (and under a certain amount of pressure, even) to support and fund evaluation activities.

Program Leadership

It should be clear from the example scenario that leadership in the French program was crucial to the evaluation project's success. Recall that the French department chair was committed to evaluation, as was a respected senior faculty member who had championed evaluation in the program for some time. Leadership is one of the most important ingredients for evaluation usefulness. If leadership is indifferent or resistant to evaluation, evaluation will have limited impact. Evaluation thrives, however, if leaders take the lead in initiating or coordinating evaluation work and if they participate in evaluation actively. Evaluation will be successful if leaders ensure there is follow-up on and use of evaluation findings. Evaluation is useful when leaders encourage participation in evaluation activities. Evaluation succeeds when leaders work to secure evaluation resources and support and address threats or barriers to evaluation practice, such as lack of funding. Evaluation is effective when leadership publicly recognizes and respects staff interested in evaluation, when they publicly support work undertaken by those interested in evaluation, and when they participate in evaluation events, workshops, or training themselves.

If readers are in a position of leadership, they should note well that evaluation use-fulness hinges on their engagement and involvement. If readers are not in a position of leadership, a concerted effort must be made to get decision-makers on board with the evaluation and—to the extent possible—bring them into the evaluation process to help plan and implement the project. Of course, some managers and program heads will be more willing than others. In cases where leaders are unavailable, they should at least be kept aware of project events and happenings via frequent communication.

Ownership

Finally, note in the French example that the motivation for the evaluation came from indi-viduals within the program. Evaluation happened because staff wanted to better under-stand and improve their teaching practices. Again, the project was not a one-off event. Evaluation had been happening cyclically for many years prior, issuing out of a culture of self-reflection, research, and evidence-based practice. This observation returns us once more to the notion of stakeholders and to two additional reasons why stakeholder involve-ment in evaluation is so important: (1) evaluation functions best when it is an ongoing activity conducted continually and cyclically by program staff and leadership, not spo-radically in response to outside pressures; and (2) evaluation seems to be most meaning-fully useful when the impetus and reason for doing evaluation originates from within the program and not as a compliance-type reaction to institutional or external requirements. A key insight from evaluation research, then—and one we want to emphasize—is that evaluation is most likely to be useful when programs energetically and consistently under-take evaluation for themselves. Of course, creating meaningful and long-lasting evaluation ownership in a language program is challenging and takes time and sustained effort (and something of a collective mind-shift). Ownership will not be achieved overnight. Yet, a successful evaluation project—using strategies from this guide—may be a key first step toward increased buy-in, incremental ownership, evidenced-based decision-making, and perhaps a future set of optimal program arrangements where evaluation realizes its poten-tial to do good in language programs.

Notes

1. Evaluation resources for language educators can be found at the AELRC website: aelrc.georgetown.edu.
2. Evaluation resources can be found at the NFLRC website: nflrc.hawaii.edu/evaluation/.

3

Planning for Useful Evaluation

Users, Uses, Questions

TODD H. McKAY and JOHN McE. DAVIS

THE STRATEGIES DESCRIBED IN the previous chapter are designed to help readers understand general best practices for conducting a successful evaluation project. In this section, we move to the key concepts of planning the evaluation project itself, and in particular, use-focused evaluation concepts that will help the project to be productively useful and achieve important program aims.

During the early stages of an evaluation, there can be a common and premature move by novice evaluators to start planning immediately for data collection. "We need a survey!" is the common refrain shortly after the project has begun. A lesson long-learned in evaluation research and practice is that deciding *how* to collect information before clarifying *who* needs to know something from the evaluation, *what* those people need to know, and *why* they need to know it leaves an evaluation project dangerously prone to collecting information decision-makers do not want or need. Evaluation in such instances fails to fulfill its potential and purpose, resources and time are wasted, and a valuable opportunity to better understand or improve language instruction through evaluative inquiry is missed.

How, then, can this state of affairs be avoided? In a use-focused approach to evaluation, three strategies are needed at this initial stage of evaluation planning:

1. Identifying and engaging specific *users* of the evaluation findings
2. Identifying users' evaluation *uses* of the evaluation information
3. Creating evaluation *questions* that capture the focus (or foci) of the evaluation project

A use-focused evaluation approach involves deliberately and explicitly clarifying each of these project components. Doing so helps ensure that the results of an evaluation are actually to make important decisions and take needed programmatic actions. This chapter discusses each of these planning components in detail.

Evaluation Users, Stakeholders

Language programs are complex. They involve many processes and components, including instructional activities, curricula, learning objectives or outcomes, assessment, teaching and learning materials, cocurricular activities, and professional development. Each of these components involves various program actors and agents, such as students, instructors, administrators, funders, program managers, alumni, and parents. In almost all educational contexts, a diverse range of individuals and entities will likely be affected by an evaluation project. Many will be impacted by the evaluation's effects and consequences. Some may have responsibility to take action on the basis of its results; others may be held accountable for program performance and the extent to which goals or outcomes are being met.

In a use-focused evaluation approach, evaluation is conducted in an intentional way to meet the needs of specific individuals. As such, part of the evaluation process involves sorting out who should or could use evaluation findings toward some programmatic or educational goal. To this end, evaluation planning requires identifying, engaging, and involving two types of program constituents: *stakeholders* and *evaluation users*.

Stakeholders

Stakeholders are people who take an interest in an educational program. They are the individuals or groups that will be affected—either directly or indirectly—by evaluation findings or actions taken on the basis of findings. There is a fundamentally democratic element to high-quality evaluation practice in that the individuals who have a stake in the language program should not be separate or excluded from the evaluation process, especially during the planning phases. Since program stakeholders are closely tied to the purposes of an evaluation, evaluation success is hindered when stakeholder perspectives are overlooked. Without stakeholder involvement, there is less understanding, appreciation, information sharing, legitimacy, or commitment to evaluation (Bryson, Patton, and Bowman 2011). By contrast, when there is stakeholder participation in evaluation, people develop project "ownership"—they care about the evaluation since it responds to their needs and priorities. If an evaluation is planned well, with active stakeholder engagement, interested parties will anticipate evaluation findings since results will shed light on things they care about. In this way, stakeholder involvement and ownership increase evaluation usefulness.

The evaluator or project team must organize participation for stakeholders throughout the evaluation project. Students (often overlooked), teachers, faculty, instructors, teaching assistants, chairs, principals, supervisors, advisors, administrators, funders, parents, future students, employers, alumni, community leaders, and others all potentially have a stake in the outcomes of an evaluation project, and the evaluator must find ways to promote stakeholder engagement (see below).

Evaluation Users

A key subgroup of stakeholders in a use-focused approach to evaluation are the evaluation "users." In a very basic sense, evaluation is a fundamentally practical activity where specific people need to take actions and make decisions to have some useful impact on a language program. Evaluation projects are never purposeless. They are always conducted by someone, for someone (or some group), to do something. An important first step in use-focused evaluation planning, then, is to explicitly identify the people who are going to do something with the evaluation project, the specific individuals who will be responsible for taking actions on the basis of results. Such individuals have a privileged role in a use-focused approach to evaluation. Ideally, they are the people for whom the evaluation is uniquely designed and whose needs are specifically served by the evaluation project.

Evaluation users are commonly individuals or groups who make decisions in the program and are in a position to use the evaluation findings to take future actions. They are also people whom Michael Quinn Patton describes as having the "personal factor"—people "who personally care about the evaluation and the findings it generates" (2008, 44). Evaluation users are interested parties and decision-makers who want or need information to better understand a particular program issue or question. Users are typically people in management or leadership positions who are accountable for program functioning and are tasked with maintaining or improving program performance. People impacted by an evaluation are stakeholders. Users are a special sub-category of stakeholders who care about the evaluation and are in a position to make programmatic decisions on the basis of results.

In the beginning stages of an evaluation, the evaluator or project team must not assume that an evaluation will meet the needs of decision-makers. Rather, a use-focused approach to evaluation calls for a concerted and intentional effort to identify the evaluation users, and to organize the evaluation in a specific way so that it will help users reach their program-development goals. Typically, evaluation planning will involve identifying and engaging with users early on, making them aware of their role and responsibilities in the evaluation (to help make decisions throughout the project), and facilitating a process where users articulate (1) what they want the evaluation to investigate (i.e., evaluation questions) and (2) how they want to use the evaluation findings (i.e., evaluation uses).

Collaborating and Communicating with Users and Stakeholders

Two additional points are important to note regarding evaluation users and stakeholders. As will become clear throughout this guide, in a use-focused evaluation approach, users must periodically participate in evaluation-planning activities and contribute to ongoing project decision-making. Again, use-focused evaluation involves tailoring evaluation to the needs of specific individuals, and doing so requires effective communication and collaboration between users and evaluators. Thus, a certain amount of commitment from users to ongoing participation is needed throughout the project.

Communication and participation are important for stakeholder groups as well. Again, involvement of stakeholders in evaluation activities leads to ownership, which increases the likelihood of evaluation usefulness. While stakeholders may not warrant as much direct involvement in project activities as users, it is still important to communicate about the project to interested parties (e.g., about project goals, data-collection activities, findings) and even organize some limited participation and project decision-making so that stakeholders buy in to the evaluation and feel it has been organized with their concerns and interests in mind. To this end, evaluators might consider ways to have stakeholders (1) help determine or prioritize evaluation uses and questions, (2) provide input on needed evaluation information, (3) assist with data collection and interpretation, and

(4) participate in action-planning for use of results. Stakeholder involvement may not be needed or appropriate at each of these steps in all contexts; nevertheless, given the importance of stakeholder input and involvement for evaluation usefulness, it is important to organize at least some stakeholder involvement and communication throughout the evaluation process.

Identifying Users and Stakeholders

With a diversity of groups and individuals involved in language programs, a process may be needed to identify stakeholders as well as the many possible candidates within stakeholder groups who have the potential to use evaluation findings. Where users and stakeholders are not straightforwardly clear—or in larger programs with complex hierarchies of stakeholder groups and power structures—*stakeholder analysis* can be a helpful tool to (1) clarify stakeholder groups and (2) identify the most appropriate candidates to be selected as evaluation users.

The power-interest grid (Mendelow 1981) in figure 3.1 can be used to determine different stakeholder groups and their potential involvement in the evaluation project. The upward-pointing arrow in figure 3.1 indicates stakeholders with more or less power within an organization. The horizontal arrow at the bottom of the figure indicates stakeholders with more and less interest in the evaluation. Where stakeholders fall along these axes in terms of their power in the organization and their likely interest in the evaluation can help to prioritize strategies for stakeholder engagement.

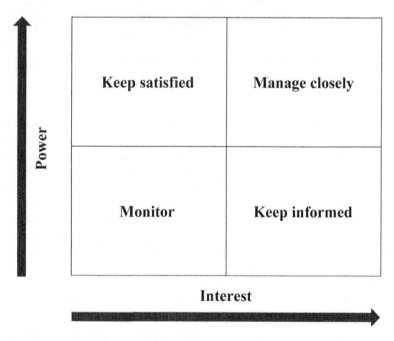

Figure 3.1 A power-interest grid to help determine stakeholder and user groups (adapted from Mendelow 1981)

For example, stakeholders with high interest and high power (in the upper-right quadrant, "manage closely") are individuals who should be kept updated on all aspects of the evaluation and potentially involved in important evaluation decision-making. An individual in this quadrant may be a director or chair who is interested in how the evaluation can help the program improve or meet accountability requirements. Accordingly, these high-interest, high-power stakeholders might be engaged by sending regular, concise emails that document the evaluation's progress or by providing brief updates during faculty meetings.

Moving to the bottom-right quadrant, those with high interest but low power ("keep informed") may be part-time instructors or faculty. They may be interested in the evaluation since findings will impact them, but they may not be in a position to impact decision-making. These stakeholders can be updated as the evaluation progresses but perhaps less frequently than those in the "manage closely" quadrant.

Stakeholders with high power and low interest (top-left quadrant, "keep satisfied") may be those in positions of authority who are perhaps only indirectly impacted by evaluation findings or busy with other tasks. This type of stakeholder might be informed of important milestones during the evaluation but may not be directly involved in project planning and subsequent decision-making.

Lastly, stakeholders in the bottom-left quadrant ("monitor"), those with low power and low interest, may be students or part-time teaching or office staff. Students and part-time staff should be informed of evaluation activities, but they are perhaps not engaged as frequently or with as much detail as a program director or other stakeholders with leadership responsibility.

Once stakeholders are arrayed in the figure to reflect their relationship to the evaluation, the diagram can be used to identify the intended evaluation users. Accordingly, those categorized in the "manage closely" quadrant will be the best candidates. Again, users are those individuals in leadership positions with the ability and desire to make program decisions. In addition, individuals within this group with the "personal factor" should be regarded as high-priority candidates. The power-analysis grid, then, can help evaluators better understand the individuals in a program or community and their relation to the evaluation project.

Evaluation Uses

When users have been identified, the next step in a use-focused evaluation approach is to determine how users will use the evaluation results once an evaluation is complete. The purpose of doing so is similar to the educational development strategy of "backward design" (Wiggins and McTighe 2005).

In backward design, before developing curricula or materials, educators first identify the targeted knowledge, skills, and dispositions they want students to achieve after a program of study. Once these are established, curriculum designers create educational experiences, course sequences, and materials—working "backward," as it were—toward the specific classroom activities and instructional strategies needed to bring about desired student learning outcomes. By thinking first about what the end result of instruction should look like—and designing a program of study with those goals in mind—the program stands a better chance of realizing its intended leaning outcomes.

Use-focused evaluation is similar. Evaluation users and evaluators must specify concretely what the evaluation will achieve—that is, what evaluation users will eventually *do* with evaluation findings—and then work backward from there, narrowing the evaluation focus and selecting data-collection tools in terms of how users intend to use the evaluation results. Through this process, evaluators design an evaluation project that has clear future goals and a road map toward those goals, both of which increase the likelihood that the evaluation will actually lead to those aims.

Getting Started: Focusing First on Evaluation Purpose

Once evaluators have determined evaluation users—and before moving to their specific uses if the project—it can be helpful to discuss in general terms why the program is conducting the evaluation project in the first place and what people generally hope to achieve. A fruitful first step, then, is to help users figure out their evaluation needs and identify their general reasons or purposes for conducting an evaluation.

Evaluation purposes are broad reasons for why evaluation generally happens in educational programs. There are a number of traditional evaluation purposes. Evaluation can be done for *formative* reasons, to make improvements, to develop a program, or to advocate for a particular course of action. Evaluations can be *summative*, to demonstrate accountability or to judge the value of a program. Or, evaluations can be *process-oriented*, to motivate, empower, or educate program stakeholders via the evaluation process itself.

In a language program, an example of a formative purpose would be a group of educators wanting to estimate the extent to which the program is meeting students' needs and wanting to make programmatic changes where students' needs are not being met. If educators wanted to judge whether a new computerized reading software is functioning successfully in the curriculum, and whether there is reason to continue funding for the software, the evaluation purpose would be a summative one. If program leadership wanted to foster evidence-based decision-making and program ownership among teachers by involving them in evaluation activities, their evaluation purpose would be process-oriented.

Knowing at the outset *why* users want to conduct an evaluation, in general terms, will guide and help narrow how evaluation findings are to be used. Asking users a few probing questions during initial discussions can uncover the general purpose for conducting an evaluation, which sets the stage for specifying particular uses (and additional users): What is the reason for this evaluation? Why is it happening? Why do people want to conduct an evaluation? What, generally, do people want to achieve with the evaluation? Is the primary aim to develop or improve the program (or some aspect of the program)? Are there any specific requirements or outside mandates for this evaluation (e.g., from funders or accreditors)?

Before proceeding further, it is worth noting that evaluation planning is rarely an orderly activity. During planning discussions, evaluators might not uncover a clear purpose in the first few meetings, or they might quickly learn there are dozens of reasons users want to conduct an evaluation. Evaluation planning at this stage is iterative, a process of "muddling through," rustling feathers, and then smoothing them. Evaluators should anticipate debate, disagreement, and a process of clarifying focus.

Identifying Evaluation Uses

With a clearer picture of why, generally, evaluation users want to conduct an evaluation, the next step is to determine how findings will be *used* once the evaluation is complete. That is, evaluators must work with evaluation users to list out the concrete actions or decisions that users will take when the evaluation results are reported. A way to help identify evaluation uses is to have users respond to the following prompt:

The findings from this evaluation will be used to _____.[1]

Responses to this statement can be a starting point for whittling down and prioritizing a *feasible* set of evaluation uses that decision-makers value and want to pursue. Note, however, that the first few ideas will likely be conceptually vague, excessively broad, too ambitious, impractical, too many in number, unrealistic, and so on. Determining a set of feasible, concrete evaluation uses often requires a number of discussions with project users. To aid in this process, the following leading statements can be offered (in a meeting or workshop) to help users conceive and articulate their uses effectively:

The findings from this evaluation will be used to _____.[2]

(1) Identify strengths and weaknesses of...
(2) Find out how well...
(3) Help faculty/instructors/students improve...
(4) Make changes to...
(5) Better understand...
(6) Demonstrate/promote the quality of...
(7) Enhance the profile of...
(8) Estimate student learning of...
(9) Come to consensus on...
(10) Validate the good work of...
(11) Justify funding/resource requests for...
(12) Develop a culture of...
(13) Meet requirements for/to...

To further aid in developing uses—and to give a sense of what evaluation uses look like for a language program evaluation—a few examples from real evaluation projects are as follows:

1. Develop procedures and materials to facilitate the induction of new, part-time Bangla-language instructors into the program.
2. Determine whether the program is preparing graduates to function effectively in university undergraduate courses.
3. Revise faculty performance-evaluation criteria to include student perspectives and feedback.
4. Explore the potential advantages and disadvantages to using class systems as an administrative course registration and management software.

A few points are important to keep in mind when developing evaluation uses. First, users can and typically will have more than one use for findings. It is entirely appropriate for an evaluation to have multiple uses, though bear in mind points above about feasibility. Furthermore, projects can have more than one user (or user group), and different users should identify different evaluation uses dedicated to their unique needs.

In addition, thinking about evaluation use should happen at *all* phases of the evaluation and not just at the beginning. The list of uses identified during planning should not be put aside until the end of the project with evaluators assuming that the evaluation will naturally lead to those ends. Rather, evaluation uses should be kept in mind at all subsequent stages of the evaluation and should inform decisions throughout the project. The tools for collecting data, the sources of information needed to answer project questions, how to report findings, and how to engage and communicate with stakeholders all depend on how evaluation findings will be used (and by whom).

For example, if a group of users wants to assess student achievement to demonstrate accountability and programmatic effectiveness to accreditors or funders, certain kinds of assessment tools will be needed that will provide persuasive evidence in the eyes of these watchful project audiences. Such needs may call for particular evaluation methods, such as tests with strong reliability and psychometric qualities, and perhaps standardized assessments backed by thorough validation. In contrast, if a group of teachers wants to collect evidence of student learning in order to shed light on the effectiveness of classroom teaching or materials, then more idiosyncratic, alternative assessment tools might be called for, possibly self-rated assessments using student questionnaires or diaries and journals. The point, then, is that establishing the ultimate uses of an evaluation is necessary not only for planning the evaluation effectively but also for informing decisions along the way so that all aspects and phases of the project are leading toward—and not away from—the desired evaluation outcomes.

Engaging in the above steps will go a long way toward ensuring an evaluation stays focused on concrete, desired aims and that there is commitment to using evaluation findings. In much the same way that language educators take pains to define what students will be able to do at the end of a lesson or program of study, so too should care be given to the explicit specification of what users intend to do with evaluation findings.

Evaluation Questions

Once users have established how findings will be used, evaluators should next develop evaluation questions. Evaluation questions are a means of focusing evaluation efforts on what users specifically want to investigate. Evaluation questions create a framework for collecting evidence and enable a systematic process of data collection, interpretation, and reporting.

Evaluation questions are developed early in evaluation planning since they help determine which data will be collected (the subject of the next chapter) and how those data will be analyzed and interpreted. There are, of course, good and not-so-good evaluation questions. Good evaluation questions share a number of important features. They should be (1) developed by users to address things they actually care about; (2) unique, in that there is not already an immediate, known answer; (3) written clearly and understandably; (4) "answerable," in that information is available to answer the question; (5) feasible, such that information to answer the question can be collected in a reasonable amount of time and with reasonable expenditure of resources; and (6) politically nonthreatening so as to avoid alienating stakeholders.

Another useful prompt that can be used with users or colleagues to help develop evaluation project questions is as follows:

What we need to know about the program is _____ .[3]

Revisiting the list of evaluation uses noted above (and keeping in mind the features of good evaluation questions), evaluators might develop evaluation questions along the lines of the following examples:

Evaluation Use	Evaluation Question
Develop procedures and materials to facilitate the induction of new, part-time Bangla-language instructors into the program.	What do new, part-time instructors need to know and be able to do in order to teach effectively in our program?
Determine whether the program is preparing graduates to function effectively in university undergraduate courses.	To what extent does our program provide graduates with the language knowledge and skills necessary to succeed in entry-level undergraduate courses?
Revise faculty performance-evaluation criteria to include student perspectives and feedback.	What type of student feedback should be incorporated into the faculty performance-evaluation process?
Explore the potential advantages and disadvantages to using a new course registration and management software.	In what ways could using a new educational management software enhance course registration and management for students?

As with evaluation uses, it is possible and appropriate for evaluation projects to have more than one evaluation question. For example, for evaluation use 2, users might also want to know, "To what extent do recent graduates *feel they were prepared* to perform successfully in their undergraduate courses?" In working to answer both questions, evaluators might gather information in multiple ways, focusing on different issues, to enable a single evaluation use. However, as noted above, the feasibility of answering multiple evaluation questions (i.e., time, money, and other resources needed to do so) should be considered carefully.

The Role of the Evaluator

We pause here to note that the emphasis on evaluation users in a use-focused evaluation approach has important implications for the role of the evaluator or project team. In a use-focused evaluation approach, the evaluator typically acts in a *support* role. That is, the use-focused evaluator conducts the project in a way that enables a key decision-maker (or decision-making group) to make judgments and decisions about the program and take action on that basis. The task and responsibility of the evaluator or team, then, is not to be the arbiter of educational effectiveness, program quality, or needed actions for improvement. Rather, the appropriate role is to *facilitate a systematic process* for an evaluation user to make such judgments. Of course, it may be (and is often the case) that instructors are simultaneously evaluators and evaluation users and that they conduct evaluation for their own educational purposes. Commonly, however, evaluation will be an activity that must respond to different users' and stakeholders' needs. To that end, the evaluator or project team must carefully plan the evaluation so that those needs are met. In this sense, evaluators act in a service role. They do what is needed to support users in achieving successful evaluation experiences, getting the information they need to make judgments about educational effectiveness, and taking actions on the basis of those judgments.

Evaluation Scenarios

Table 3.1 lists possible stakeholders, users, uses, and questions for each of the evaluation scenarios. Of course, many alternatives are possible. Ultimately, these planning elements will be determined by the needs and desires of stakeholders in a specific educational context. It is the job of the evaluator to ensure that these elements are in place and, crucially, that there is clarity and stakeholder input on *why* the evaluation is happening—and for *whom*—prior to deciding *how* the program will be evaluated.

Notes

1. Adapted from Patton (2008).
2. Ibid.
3. Ibid.

Table 3.1 Stakeholders, users, uses, and questions for evaluation scenarios

Scenario 1	Stakeholders	Users	Uses	Questions
Community College Language Lab	Dean, Division of Liberal Arts	Chair of the humanities division	Better understand how well the lab supports the language-learning needs of lab users	How well is the language lab supporting language education at the college?
	Chair, Department of Humanities	Lab coordinator	Identify the range of needs, uses, and users the lab does not support currently	What changes or innovations are needed to better support lab users and campus stakeholders?
	Lab coordinator, staff	Lab staff	Identify needed improvements and changes given current and future needs of lab users	
	Instructors/Faculty			
	Students		Demonstrate the value of technology-mediated language learning to the campus community	
	Lab coordinators at local colleges			

Scenario 2	Stakeholders	Users	Uses	Questions
Adult Language Program Needs Analysis	Program director	Program director	Identify language-learning needs of English language students working in the community and local economy	What are the language-learning needs of English language students at the center?
	Students	Curriculum committee	Make changes to the curriculum on the basis of identified needs	How well is the current curriculum providing the language skills students need to work and live in their communities?
	Faculty			
	Curriculum committee			
	Assessment coordinator			
	Local employers			

Scenario 3	Stakeholders	Users	Uses	Questions
Eleventh-grade Chinese Telecollaboration	Teachers at both schools (at various grade levels)	School principal	Better understand the impact of the telecollaboration program on student language development	How satisfied are students and teachers with the telecollaboration program?
	Students at both schools	Teachers at both schools	Identify programmatic areas in need of improvement and modification	How effective is the Chinese telecollaboration program for student learning?
	Administrators, coordinators, principals, etc. at both schools		Demonstrate the effectiveness of the program to parents and other educational stakeholders	
	Parents			
	State educational officers			

4

Identifying Indicators for Evaluation Data Collection

FRANCESCA VENEZIA

THE NEXT STEP IN evaluation planning is to decide how to collect information for the evaluation. More specifically, evaluators will need to carefully identify the relevant information needed to answer evaluation questions and to enable decision-makers to use the evaluation in the ways they desire. However, evaluators must still resist the urge to select the data-collection tools that seem appropriate for collecting relevant information (e.g., questionnaires, interviews, assessments, etc.). Rather, an important prior step is necessary to help ensure users get the *specific types* of information they need to answer their evaluation questions. This intervening step involves identifying evaluation "indicators," or the different sources of evidence that will be measured, captured, or otherwise described in order to shed light on how the program is performing or functioning.

In a simple sense, an indicator is a type of information or evidence needed to answer an evaluation question. For example, consider the following fictional evaluation question: "To what extent is the new, task-based teaching approach helpful for student learning?" To answer this question, one can imagine that there would be something happening in classrooms or elsewhere in the program—in terms of student behavior, performance, or some other phenomena—that would be suggestive of whether task-based teaching activities were helping students learn. That is, something in the program would "indicate" whether learning from task-based instruction was happening or not. Along these lines, a useful way to think about (and identify) indicators is to ask, "How will we know?" in conjunction with a particular evaluation question. For example, a way of conceptualizing an evaluation indicator for the evaluation question above would be to further ask, "How will we know the extent to which the new task-based teaching approach is helpful for student learning?" What would the answer to this question be? What would evidence of "helpfulness for student learning" look like? Some possible answers are the following:

- Amount of interaction and negotiation happening during task-based classroom activities[1]
- Level of student motivation and interest during task-based activities

- Student ability to successfully conduct important, task-based learning outcomes (e.g., writing a paragraph, asking for and understanding directions)
- Ability to complete educational or professional tasks in real-life contexts

Each of the above phenomena would arguably provide important insights into the extent to which task-based instruction was impacting student learning in helpful ways. For example, increased negotiation between students during classroom interactions is known to have important language-learning benefits, and if measured or assessed in some way, could well be regarded as indicating a helpful impact on learning from task-based language teaching. Likewise for motivation, which is known to increase when students engage in interesting tasks related to their language-learning needs. The same could be argued for successful completion of important task-based, course-learning outcomes or evidence from real-life contexts that students are better able to complete work- or education-related tasks—both, arguably, would be suggestive that a task-based approach had helped students' language development.

Again, an indicator expresses what will be measured, captured, or otherwise described in order to answer an evaluation question. Identifying and listing indicators for each evaluation question is a specific strategy to help make evaluation more useful. The process of identifying indicators acts as a check against collecting the wrong type of evaluation information or selecting data-collection tools that capture information in nonuseful ways (points developed next). After determining evaluation questions and uses, evaluation planning should involve a collaborative process where stakeholders, users, and evaluators work together to identify the indicators for the evaluation prior to deciding how that information will be captured.

Indicators versus Data-Collection Methods

As hinted already, an indicator is *not* the same thing as a data-collection method. Recalling the evaluation question above, evaluators and users might be tempted to think that a questionnaire will indicate whether the task-based teaching approach is helping students learn. In one sense, this is true. However, it is important to understand that a questionnaire is not an indicator. It is, rather, a tool that reveals the indicator, or reveals some aspect of the task-based program suggestive of its helpfulness for learning. That is, a questionnaire is a data-collection strategy used to find out about something going on in the program that sheds light on whether task-based instruction is developing student learning (i.e., the indicator).

Data-collection tools, then, capture indicators. To illustrate this point using the example indicators noted above, an observation checklist completed by an instructor would capture the extent to which negotiation is happening during in-class communication; a student questionnaire would shed light on student motivation during task-based activities; different types of assessment would capture student ability to successfully perform important tasks or learning outcomes at the end of a course; and interviews with employers or workplace colleagues would help to better understand graduates' abilities to complete work-related tasks in real-life contexts.

The distinction between indicators versus evaluation data-collection methods or tools is an intentional one in evaluation practice and serves an important purpose in helping to support evaluation usefulness. Separating indicators and data-collection methods helps to ensure that evaluation users collect relevant information needed for their evaluation uses. How does identifying indicators achieve this aim? As discussed, a common occurrence in evaluation is for stakeholders to initially think about *how* to collect information instead of why, for whom, and to what ends. Again, a frequent instinct is to decide at the outset that a questionnaire will be needed for data collection. While this may end up being the case, it is important to understand that questionnaires (and other tools) collect information in particular ways—ways that are well-suited to some evaluation purposes but potentially ill-suited to others (see chapters 6–8). Selecting the wrong tool can result in capturing the wrong type of information. For example, if a group of educators wanted to evaluate how well a curriculum was meeting student needs, stakeholders and evaluators would likely want to generate and collect new, previously unknown ideas about student language needs relevant to their professional goals. If a questionnaire were selected for this purpose, it might not succeed since—all things being equal—questionnaires are good for collecting information from respondents about *known* issues or ideas (e.g., via ratings of items for agreement, importance, usefulness, etc.). Questionnaires tend not to be the best way to have respondents generate new information, which would be needed in a project trying to identify students' language needs. Were an evaluation team to prematurely develop and administer a questionnaire in this example, they might fail to collect the information needed for users' program-development aims.

Before jumping to a questionnaire or any other data-collection tool, then, it pays to first ask, "What *sort* of information is needed?" and once this is known, choose data-collection tools accordingly. Different data-collection methods provide different perspectives and tell different stories about what is going on in a program. Some stories will be what users want to hear given what they want to do with evaluation information. Other stories will fail to provide the right information. Thinking more abstractly about the types of evidence (i.e., the indicators) needed for an evaluation project helps to ensure that relevant evidence is collected for particular users for particular uses. Considering the student needs-analysis example, an indicator for this scenario might be the "education-related tasks that students perform during study abroad," in which case interviews or focus groups involving a variety of informants might be better suited to generating the types of information needed for program-development purposes. If there is too much focus on methods early on, it is possible to lose sight of evaluation goals, and relevant data sources can be missed.

Developing Useful Indicators: SPICED

A number of steps and strategies can be used to help end-users identify and develop high-quality indicators. To aid in this process, Lennie et al. (2011) have proposed the acronym SPICED, a mnemonic to help evaluators and stakeholders create strong indicators that contribute to evaluation usefulness:

S = Subjective
P = Participatory
I = Interpreted
C = Cross-checked
E = Empowering
D = Diverse

Being *subjective* during the identification of indicators means taking into consideration users' opinions and insights into the program and the information that will make most sense to them. Indicators can be conceived in different ways, and different indicators can be used to shed light on a single evaluation question. However, different stakeholders value different types of evidence. No set of indicators is applicable in all program contexts, so users need to identify and select those indicators that make sense to them.

Creating indicators in a *participatory* way builds on the idea of subjectivity in that the identification of indicators should happen in collaboration with evaluation users and other stakeholders. Again, useful evaluation involves giving users the information they need for their program-development or decision-making needs. Indicators need to be perceived as appropriate and accurate by those who will do something with evaluation information, otherwise methods decisions may be questioned and findings seen as untrustworthy. Indicators, then, should be negotiated and approved by decision-makers and other key stakeholders.

Indicators should also be *interpretable* by users and stakeholders. "Interpretable" means that indicators must be understandable to all those involved in the evaluation. Esoteric, technical indicators involving, say, inferential statistics (e.g., results of time-series regression analyses) will fail to be useful if users cannot understand what the indicator suggests about program functioning or performance.

Next, where feasible and appropriate to do so, indicators should be *cross-checked*; that is, different indicators should triangulate the same source of information. Triangulation will not always be possible or necessary, but different perspectives on a single program element or phenomena can be an important consideration in high-stakes projects where evaluation must meet high standards of data trustworthiness.

Empowering refers to identifying and developing indicators in a way that offers an opportunity for reflection and enables those involved in the evaluation to effect change in their program. Considering *diversity* in the creation of indicators involves gathering input from different program stakeholders and user groups who bring different views and knowledge to the table. Representing a diversity of views in evaluation decisions increases the likelihood that a range of program stakeholders will see evaluation results as relevant and trustworthy.

Developing Useful Indicators: Considering Program Context

Additional considerations for creating high-quality indicators relate to the conditions and constraints placed upon an evaluation in the particular context where the evaluation is taking place. That is, the creation of indicators will be affected by (1) resources available for data collection, (2) time frames for the evaluation project, and (3) evaluation users' knowledge and background (Patton 2008).

Clearly, availability of resources will affect the kind of data that can be collected. For example, consider the indicator "ability to complete tasks in real-life contexts." Various factors will impact data collection for this indicator. Are alumni tracked after they leave the program? Does accurate contact information exist? Can different assessments be conducted to estimate students' real-world language use? How accessible are supervisors, managers, or other informants to comment on graduates' language abilities? Addressing these issues may require a special outlay of resources, and if so, their availability will affect data collection. If resources do not exist, the indicator may need to be worded differently or sacrificed altogether in order to conduct a feasible evaluation project that stands a chance of actually being completed.

Time frames are another consideration. Evaluation projects often need to be conducted in a short period of time, and if so, indicators must be worded in a way that reflects this constraint. For example, it can often be the case that short-term indicators have to be used to predict long-term results. In such instances, if, say, stakeholders want to know to what extent the program is improving students' language skills and the evaluation time frame does not permit assessing students throughout the program, beginning and interim linguistic gains may have to suffice as an indicator of learning development instead of end-of-program gains. That said, short-term indicators may fail to garner attention from stakeholders or capture relevant information. For example, the effect of a new teacher-training program may require tracking assessment results over a longer time period and looking for trends in student performance before and after the introduction of the training program.

Lastly, and importantly, evaluation users' knowledge and background need to be considered when creating indicators. Evaluation users know the program best; they have unique knowledge and insight about the program. They know what information is available. They can advise on feasibility and appropriate time frames. They may also have previous evaluation experience, which can provide valuable information. In addition, evaluation users should be active in the identification of indicators since their involvement increases ownership and the likelihood that indicators will be meaningful, thereby increasing the likelihood of use. Just as evaluation users should be involved in the creation of evaluation questions and uses (see chapter 3), they should also be active in creating indicators, and for the same reason—ownership is created when users feel their needs and interests are being addressed.

Performance Measurement

We briefly note that the term "indicator" is also important for a specific type of evaluative activity common in educational evaluation known as "performance measurement." Performance measurement is similar to evaluation in the sense that it involves systematic data-collection for decision-making purposes, though the term refers more narrowly to the ongoing monitoring of program performance and the extent to which a program is meeting its goals or objectives.

Performance measurement typically involves some variety of the following processes or activities:

1. Setting program goals and/or objectives that capture the essential aims of the program.
2. Establishing "performance indicators" as a means of gauging programmatic goal or outcome attainment. For example, were a school to set a program outcome that "graduating students develop job-related language abilities to gain employment," a performance indicator or evidence of whether this outcome was being attained might be the number of graduating students finding employment after completing

language training. The extent to which the program is achieving this outcome (i.e., its performance) is "measured" by tracking the number of students who are successful in finding employment.

3. Setting a performance benchmark or target as a marker of achievement; for example, seventy percent of students finding employment out of each graduating cohort.

4. Periodically collecting information on the indicator and comparing results against the benchmark to estimate the extent to which a program is attaining or falling short of its targets (and taking programmatic actions where necessary).

In this way, the program "measures" its performance and collects evidence as to whether it is meeting its goals and objectives. Indicators in this framework are still expressions of what will be measured, captured, or otherwise described, though they are primarily for the purpose of monitoring performance trends in a wrong or right direction. We note that the now-common requirement for language instructors to engage in "outcomes assessment" at junior colleges and universities is a version of this process in that postsecondary institutions now mandate that all departments and cocurricular education programs assess and track student performance. Providing advice on outcomes assessment or performance measurement in language programs goes beyond the scope of this book, though the advice in this chapter also applies to the development of performance indicators in performance-measurement frameworks, as well as to assessment of student learning outcomes in language departments at colleges and universities.

Indicators for Evaluation Scenarios

Table 4.1 is a continuation of table 3.1 from chapter 3. Here, we add example indicators to each scenario to give a sense of how these might be conceived and worded in an evaluation project plan. Of course, many other indicators will be possible in addition to those noted here, though the quality and usefulness of any of the scenario indicators will depend on the factors discussed above. Most importantly, however, indicators should be approved by evaluation users.

Note

1. Negotiation of meaning refers to communication breakdowns and repairs during meaningful interaction known to be useful for language development.

● Table 4.1 Scenarios: Evaluation questions and indicators

Scenario 1	Evaluation question	Indicator ("How will we know?")
Community College Language Lab	1. How well is the language lab supporting language education at the college?	1. Number/frequency of lab visitors
		2. Type of lab visitor
		3. Most and least frequent uses of the language lab by visitors and staff
		4. Most and least frequently used lab equipment or technology
		5. Use of lab space by lab visitors
		6. Usefulness of resources, equipment/technology, spaces for campus stakeholders
		7. Satisfaction with resources, equipment/technology, spaces by campus stakeholders
		8. Deterrents to lab use or visitation
	2. What changes or innovations are needed to better support lab users and campus stakeholders?	1. Desired uses of the lab by users, staff, and campus stakeholders
		2. Desired lab equipment/technology by users, staff, and campus stakeholders
		3. Desired spaces by users, staff, and campus stakeholders
		4. Best practices in language labs, media centers at peer institutions
		5. Best practices in media-center activities, innovation, and support at US colleges and universities

(continued)

● **Table 4.1** Scenarios: Evaluation questions and indicators (*continued*)

Scenario 2	Evaluation question	Indicator ("How will we know?")
Adult Language Program Needs Analysis	1. What are the language-learning needs of English language students at the center?	1. Key tasks in local professional and educational English situations
		2. Desired language skills/abilities by employers
		3. Felt language-learning needs by students
		4. What program alumni can/cannot do in English in professional and educational contexts
	2. How well is the current curriculum providing the language skills students need to work and live in their communities?	1. Alignment of program/course objectives with student language-learning needs
		2. Correspondence between curricula, materials, and instructional activities and students' learning needs
		3. Correspondence between pedagogical approach and students' learning needs
		4. Alignment of assessment/testing with language-learning needs
		5. Similarities and discrepancies between student abilities developed in the program and targeted language needs
		6. Performance of alumni in relevant professional and educational contexts

Scenario 3	Evaluation question	Indicator ("How will we know?")
Eleventh-grade Chinese Telecollaboration	1. How satisfied are students and teachers with the telecollaboration program?	1. Satisfaction with the program by students, teachers, staff, parents
		2. Perceived usefulness of telecollaboration program for student learning
		3. Student motivation, engagement during telecollaboration sessions
		4. Intention to pursue future Chinese study by program participants
		5. Enrollment of telecollaboration participants in twelfth-grade Chinese courses
	2. How effective is the Chinese telecollaboration program for student learning?	1. Level of Chinese language ability and attainment of learning outcomes at the end of the telecollaboration program
		2. Performance in regular eleventh-grade Chinese courses: Chinese telecollaboration students' course achievement versus non-telecollaboration Chinese students

5

Selecting Methods and Collecting Data for Evaluation

TODD H. McKAY and JOHN McE. DAVIS

AT THIS STAGE IN an evaluation project, substantial planning work has been done to help increase the likelihood that evaluation findings are useful for programmatic decision-making. Specifically, planning efforts will have led to evaluators, users, and stakeholders identifying the following:

1. Specifically who needs to do something via the evaluation (i.e., the evaluation users)
2. What those groups or individuals need to do with evaluation information (i.e., the evaluation uses)
3. Specifically what they want to investigate (i.e., the evaluation questions)
4. The types of information needed to "answer" the evaluation questions (i.e., the indicators)

Ideally, all of these steps will have preceded decisions about specifically how data will be collected or which tools will be used to collect needed information. As argued in chapter 4, the purpose of doing so is to avoid common evaluation planning mistakes (i.e., choosing the wrong tools or not choosing enough tools) and to ensure that the right information is collected given project users' needs.

These planning steps completed, evaluators can now select—and help users select—the specific strategies for collecting evaluation information. Questionnaires, focus groups, interviews, assessments, document review, photos, videos, expert panels, simulations, journals, logs, diaries, observation, testimonials, and so on are all possible choices. Of course, each method has its strengths and weaknesses (see chapters 6–8). Different data-collection methods provide specific types of information, which shed light on evaluation questions in different ways. Questionnaires, for example, can collect information from large numbers of respondents, which can be analyzed relatively quickly and efficiently, though results from selected-response items may provide little insight into program processes. By contrast, interview or focus-group information may provide nuanced insights into complex program processes, though the full scope of the textual-type data can be difficult to summarize and report in a parsimonious way. In addition to the strengths and weaknesses of particular tools affecting methods decisions, stakeholders and users might privilege certain types of information over others (e.g., textual over numerical or statistical), which may argue for choosing one tool over another. Or practical considerations, like time and expertise, may impact which tool is possible or feasible to use (assessment, for example, can require specialized expertise).

Choosing the most appropriate data-collection tool, then, will depend on a number of considerations, not the least of which is the ultimate aim of providing users with the information they need to realize their intended evaluation uses. To that end, evaluators will need to consider various factors to ensure that the right tools are selected:

1. Matching the tool to an indicator
2. Trustworthy information
3. Feasibility, practicality
4. Qualitative, quantitative, or mixed methods
5. Ethical data collection and evaluation
6. Engaging users in methods choices

Matching the Tool to an Indicator

When selecting a data-collection tool, evaluators need to ensure that the tool or strategy captures evidence directly related to project indicators. This point cannot be stressed enough. Every tool selected for an evaluation should demonstrably link to one or more project indicators. Any tool that fails to collect information on an indicator should be eliminated from the project plan since it will likely fail to collect information relevant to the evaluation questions. A matrix, like the one depicted in table 5.1, should be a part of every evaluation plan and should lay out in a systematic way which tools are being used to capture which indicators.

Trustworthy Information

For evaluation to be useful, users and other stakeholders need to have confidence in the evaluation results and conclusions. Data collection, then, needs to be conducted in a way that users regard as trustworthy. Users need to view the tools and strategies selected for their evaluation as appropriate to their aims and intended uses. Data trustworthiness corresponds to the research notion of validity and the different ways in which bias, measurement error, and other types of inaccuracy can creep into methods-design and data-collection processes.

Trustworthy data collection means that tools and strategies capture information accurately. That is, evaluation tools and strategies should not distort or otherwise change the information they intend to capture because of faulty design or implementation. For example, poorly written questionnaire items may influence respondents to answer in ways that they might not have otherwise had the item been written differently (e.g., in a more neutral way). Or, an interviewer who shows excessive disapproval or enthusiasm during an interview may change how the interviewee responds, resulting in the evaluation collecting information that is to some extent changed by the interviewer's behavior. Chapters 6, 7, and 8 provide advice on how to design and implement questionnaires, focus groups, and interviews in ways that capture information systematically and reduce bias and other types of measurement error.

Of course, no data-collection tool or strategy is fully free of bias, nor does any tool (or set of tools) perfectly capture the objective reality of a viewpoint, ability, or program process. Furthermore, in the world of academic research, there are strong opinions about what it is possible and not possible to know using the range of data-collection techniques currently available for investigating human actors in social situations. Some evaluation users may have strong views about what constitutes accurate, trustworthy, valid, or reliable information and the data-collection strategies needed to collect that information. It is important, then, that tools appear trustworthy and appropriate on the "face" of things for their intended uses in the eyes of evaluation users. It is the responsibility of the evaluator to check that users trust the evaluation methods and the overall plan for data collection.

Another trustworthiness concern has to do with whether the evidence used for the evaluation reflects trends and processes in the program. Even if tools are capturing data accurately, they may not be capturing enough data, or they may be capturing idiosyncratic data that do not correspond to what is happening in the program. This issue is particularly relevant when collecting information from informants and relates to whether the views of the individuals captured in the evaluation correspond to the views of similar individuals (or some other unit of observation) in the program. The concern with trustworthiness in this instance has less to do with bias or inaccuracy within the tool itself and more with the process of selecting informants. Commonly, users will be interested in the extent to which information collected in the evaluation generalizes to what is going on in the program. For example, if student or instructor questionnaire data is used, there will be interest in whether the questionnaire results reflect the views of students or instructors who did not complete the questionnaire. Users commonly want to know if everyone in the program shares the views reported in the evaluation findings. Evaluators thus need to consider issues of sampling, representativeness, and whether results generalize beyond themselves to a similar responding group or population of units. Continuing with the questionnaire example, if evaluators sent the questionnaire to alumni and only ten percent responded, the small numbers of respondents may not have captured enough information to reflect the views of all alumni. Rather, the results would reflect the views of the smaller responding group only, perhaps the more annoyed or more enthusiastic respondents. When results like this are reported at the end of an evaluation, users and decision-makers are quick to spot and point out lacking representativeness. And when they do, the trustworthiness and usefulness of the results—and the evaluation generally—are badly undermined. Approaches to sampling go beyond the scope of this guide,[1] but we strongly urge readers to be mindful of data representativeness and the ways in which users might question whether results correspond to what everyone is thinking—and what is really happening—in the program.

Feasibility, Practicality
Some other important factors to consider in choosing data-collection tools are practical in nature, such as available resources, intrusiveness of methods, or data-collection expertise. Careful attention to constraints on resources and time will help ensure that

data collection proceeds as efficiently as possible. To this end, evaluators should first take stock of what resources are available for data collection as early in the planning stages as possible. Resources may include things like the availability of a team member with the necessary expertise for analyzing statistical or comments data; the time needed to conduct and transcribe interviews and focus groups; or the availability of classroom or office space for interviews and focus groups.

In addition, evaluators should consider whether (and how much) training is needed to facilitate data-collection tasks. For example, the quality of comments data (from interviews or focus groups) depends on the quality of the data-collection process. Poor interviewing techniques and bad questions are unlikely to provide high-quality data. Therefore, recognize whether training is needed, how much, and what resources can be put aside to make it happen.

Qualitative, Quantitative, or Mixed Methods?

Another factor to consider is the type of information that end-users will regard as sufficiently trustworthy for their evaluation needs and uses. Broadly speaking, information collected from different tools can be textual (qualitative) or numerical and statistical (quantitative). The perceived differences between these two types of data and the merits of the research paradigms they represent have been debated among researchers and evaluation practitioners for many years. Some—arguing from the qualitative side—hold that aspects of the lived human experience cannot be categorized, defined, or fully understood in terms of numbers and experimental methods, while those on the quantitative side argue that subjective descriptions of phenomena fail to capture anything meaningfully objective about social situations (among other points of contention).

Like others in the program evaluation field, we suggest a practical position in this debate. We suggest that given the practical, evaluation-related aim of taking concrete programmatic actions, both approaches to "knowing" about a program bring something different and worthwhile to an evaluation and can be used in tandem to meet various ends. Since no one type of information can shed light on all possible evaluation questions, a use-focused evaluation approach emphasizes a *mixed-methodological* approach, using both qualitative and quantitative information types. Ultimately, evaluation is a practical endeavor that seeks to improve, better understand, or determine the value of the program of interest. All things being equal, different data-collection methods and combinations of different information types provide the richest perspective on program phenomena.

Ethical Data Collection and Evaluation

One important consideration when collecting evaluation data is to be mindful of the rights and well-being of individuals involved in or impacted by the evaluation, particularly those supplying information via focus groups, interviews, or questionnaires. Evaluation and research overlap in this respect in that both involve collecting information from human subjects who expose themselves to risk of harm by participating in research or evaluation activities. As such, it is an important responsibility for the evaluator to meet certain standards of ethical evaluation practice and ensure that there are no unintended harmful consequences for individuals participating in the evaluation project.

A useful and relevant source of information providing guidance on ethical evaluation practice is the *Program Evaluation Standards* from the Joint Committee on Standards for Educational Evaluation (Yarbrough et al. 2011). Two of the "propriety" standards are especially germane to interaction with human subjects during evaluation activities:

- Rights of Human Subjects: Evaluations should be designed and conducted to respect and protect the rights and welfare of human subjects.
- Human Interactions: Evaluators should respect human dignity and worth in their interactions with other persons associated with an evaluation so participants are not threatened or harmed.

Before collecting data from human informants, we urge readers to familiarize themselves with the propriety standards as well as seek advice from any local internal review board or like entity that provides guidelines for collecting information on human subjects for research or educational purposes. Program evaluation is not typically regarded as "research" and commonly does not come under regulations for human subjects review. Nevertheless, we urge readers to adopt best evaluation practices and be mindful of participants' well-being during and after evaluation activities. To these ends, we recommend the following guidelines when collecting information from evaluation informants:

- Informants provide informed consent to participate in data-collection activities.
- The entity or persons conducting the evaluation are stated clearly.
- The purpose of data collection is explained.
- How informants' responses will be used in the evaluation is explained.
- The steps taken to protect informant privacy are explained.
- Participants are allowed to withdraw from the evaluation at any time and have their responses withdrawn as well.

Engaging Users in Choosing Methods

Deciding which tools to select for the evaluation is the responsibility of *two* parties during evaluation planning: evaluators and users. Choosing data methods is a particularly vulnerable point in the evaluation process that can make or break usefulness. While we have stated that, all things being equal, a mixed-methods design is the best way to capture rich evaluation data, this prescription must be weighed against users' preferences for specific types of information. Again, some users may prefer numbers, statistics, and a quantitatively rendered summary of the program. Other users may privilege text, commentary, testimonial, and a more narrative-type program picture. Thus, in addition to the considerations noted above, the choice of which type of information to collect must also be guided by what users regard as most persuasively trustworthy.

Evaluators must not make decisions about methods without the review and approval of users. Getting this approval will involve engaging with users during evaluation planning to select or develop tools they regard as best suited to the evaluation purpose and most enabling of their evaluation uses. Ideally, sitting down with users and collaboratively making methods decisions is the optimal scenario.

In addition, Patton (2008) suggests an innovative way to engage users in methods decisions that involves presenting users with fictional results from a few proposed data-collection tools and asking users what they would do were the results real. Evaluators can provide mock bar charts, tables, and other types of data visualization to give users a sense of the types of information that are likely to come out of the evaluation. Monitoring user reactions to the various options can highlight any issues or problems they might have with the existing data collection plan.

If, however, a meeting is not possible, at the very least evaluators must submit the data-collection plan to users and explicitly ask for their review and approval. Again, one of the most common ways that evaluations fail is when users find fault with some aspect of data collection, be it a type of method, a type of information, or the representativeness and generalizability of results. It is crucially important, then, that users approve the strategies and plans for data collection before data collection begins.

Evaluation Scenarios

Table 5.1 continues to build on the evaluation planning for the three program scenarios. In addition to the original set of evaluation questions and indicators provided in chapters 3 and 4, a third column is added that lists the data-collection methods that could be used in each scenario. A fourth column lists the sources or types of informant that will be targeted. Note that these are only a subset of possible methods that could be used to elicit the indicators determined by end-users in each scenario. These are not the only methods that the evaluation team could employ. Other options are possible. The choice of data-collection methods is variable and depends on collaboration with, and feedback from, evaluation users. Data-collection methods listed here are meant primarily to illustrate the iterative process of evaluation work and the mapping of indicators to methods.

Questionnaires, Interviews, Focus Groups

With an understanding of how to select data-collection methods, the next task is to review the different options for data collection, the types of information they provide, and some of the indicators they are most apt to capture. The most common data-collection methods employed in language program evaluation tend to be assessments, observations, interviews, focus groups, and questionnaires. The next three chapters address three of the most commonly used data-collection methods: interviews, focus groups, and questionnaires. Each requires a certain amount of familiarity and training to collect high-quality data. As such, the following chapters provide readers with detailed advice on designing and implementing each of these data-collection methods in ways that contribute to evaluation usefulness in language programs.

Note

1. For more information on sampling, refer to Davis (2015).

● Table 5.1 Data-collection methods for evaluation scenarios

Scenario 1	Evaluation question	Indicator ("How will we know?")	Method	Informant/Source
Community College Language Lab	How well is the language lab supporting language education at the college?	1. Number/Frequency of lab visitors	● Document analysis	● Lab records of number of visitors
		2. Type of lab visitor	● Questionnaire	● Lab visitors
		3. Most and least frequent uses of the language lab by visitors and staff	● Focus group ● Questionnaire ● Interview	● Lab visitors ● Lab visitors ● Lab staff
		4. Most and least frequently used lab equipment or technology	● Focus group ● Questionnaire ● Interview	● Lab visitors ● Lab visitors ● Lab staff
		5. Use of lab space by lab visitors	● Focus group ● Interview	● Lab visitors ● Lab staff
		6. Usefulness of current lab resources, equipment or technology, and spaces for campus stakeholders	● Focus group ● Questionnaire ● Interview	● Lab visitors ● Lab visitors ● Faculty, lab staff
		7. Satisfaction with lab resources, equipment or technology, and spaces by campus stakeholders	● Focus group ● Questionnaire ● Interview	● Lab visitors ● Lab visitors ● Faculty, lab staff
		8. Deterrents to lab use or visitation	● Focus group ● Interview	● Lab visitors ● Faculty, lab staff

(continued)

● Table 5.1 Data-collection methods for evaluation scenarios *(continued)*

Scenario 1	Evaluation question	Indicator ("How will we know?")	Method	Informant/Source
Community College Language Lab (continued)	What changes or innovations are needed to better support lab users and campus stakeholders?	1. Desired uses of the language lab by users, staff, and campus stakeholders	● Focus group ● Questionnaire ● Interview	● Lab visitors ● Lab visitors ● Faculty, lab staff, administrators
		2. Desired lab equipment or technology by users, staff, and campus stakeholders	● Focus group ● Questionnaire ● Interview	● Lab visitors ● Lab visitors ● Faculty, lab staff, administrators
		3. Desired spaces by users, staff, and campus stakeholders	● Focus group ● Questionnaire ● Interview	● Lab visitors ● Lab visitors ● Faculty, lab staff, administrators
		4. Best practices in college language labs and media centers at peer institutions	● Interview	● Lab directors at peer institutions
		5. Best practices in media-center activities, innovation, and support at US colleges and universities	● Literature review	● Published research studies

Scenario 2	Evaluation question	Indicator ("How will we know?")	Method	Informant/Source
Adult Language Program Needs Analysis	What are the language-learning needs of English language students at the center?	1. Key tasks in professional and educational English language situations	• Focus group • Questionnaire • Document review	• Instructors • Program director, coordinators • Curricular documents of peer programs; relevant literature and studies on immigrant language ESL needs and instruction
		2. Desired language skills/abilities by employers	• Interview	• Key local employers
		3. Felt language-learning needs by students	• Focus group • Questionnaire	• Students • Students
		4. What program alumni can and cannot do in English in professional and educational contexts	• Questionnaire • Interview	• Alumni • Employers
	How well is the current curriculum providing the language skills students need to work and live in their communities?	1. Alignment of program/course learning objectives with student language-learning needs	• Focus group • Interview • Document review	• Instructors • Program director, coordinators • Objectives statements
		2. Correspondence between curricula, materials, and instructional activities and students' learning needs	• Focus group • Interview • Document review	• Instructors • Program director, coordinators • Objectives statements
		3. Correspondence between pedagogical approach and students' learning needs	• Focus group • Interview • Observation	• Instructors • Program director, coordinators • Classroom teaching

(continued)

● Table 5.1 Data-collection methods for evaluation scenarios (*continued*)

Scenario 2	Evaluation question	Indicator ("How will we know?")	Method	Informant/Source
Adult Language Program Needs Analysis (continued)	How well is the current curriculum providing the language skills students need to work and live in their communities? (continued)	4. Alignment of assessment/testing with language-learning needs	● Focus group ● Interview ● Document review	● Instructors ● Program director, coordinators ● Assessment tools
		5. Similarities and discrepancies between student abilities developed in the program and targeted language needs	● Focus group ● Interview ● Assessment	● Instructors ● Program chairs, director ● Student test scores, portfolios, class products of student performance
		6. Performance of alumni in relevant professional and educational contexts	● Questionnaire ● Interview	● Alumni ● Employers

Scenario 3	Evaluation question	Indicator ("How will we know?")	Method	Informant/Source
Eleventh-grade Chinese Telecollaboration	How satisfied are students and teachers with the telecollaboration program?	1. Felt satisfaction with the program by students, teachers, staff, parents	● Focus group ● Questionnaire ● Interview	● Students, parents ● Students ● Instructors, staff
		2. Perceived usefulness of the telecollaboration program for student learning	● Focus group ● Questionnaire ● Interview	● Students, parents ● Students ● Instructors
		3. Motivation, engagement during telecollaboration sessions	● Focus group ● Questionnaire ● Interview ● Observation	● Students ● Students ● Instructors ● Classroom activities

	Questionnaire	Students
4. Intention to pursue future Chinese study by program participants	Questionnaire	Students
5. Enrollment of telecollaboration participants in twelfth-grade Chinese courses	Document review	Enrolment records

How effective is the Chinese telecollaboration program for student learning?	1. Level of Chinese language ability and attainment of learning outcomes at the end of the telecollaboration program	Questionnaire, Interview, Assessment	Students, Instructors, Course assessment portfolio; Mandarin STAMP 4S*
	2. Performance in regular eleventh-grade Chinese courses: Chinese telecollaboration students' course achievement versus non-telecollaboration Chinese students	Assessment	End-of-semester Chinese course proficiency and achievement assessment

* Avant STAMP (STAndards-based Measurement of Proficiency) 4S is a web-based proficiency assessment of reading, writing, listening, and speaking abilities for grades 7–16 (https://avantassessment.com/stamp4s).

6

Conducting Focus Groups for Evaluation

LARA BRYFONSKI

WITH THE ARRAY OF data-collection techniques at the disposal of an evaluator or evaluation team, it is necessary to take careful consideration of each tool's advantages and drawbacks when deciding how to best elicit the information needed to answer evaluation questions. One such data-collection technique, focus groups, has the potential to elicit rich detail and in-depth descriptions that take the opinions and desires of stakeholders into consideration (Grudens-Schuck, Larson, and Allen 2004).

The following chapter first defines and describes focus groups and then identifies possible advantages and disadvantages in using this data-collection technique for evaluation purposes. Next, the relevant steps in planning, moderating, and implementing focus groups are discussed, including tips for developing a clear sequence of prompts as well as key aspects of data collection and analysis. Finally, the chapter ends with issues related to language program evaluation in particular, such as working with multilingual participants, translation, and participant confidentiality.

Defining Focus Groups

A focus group is a particular type of group discussion or group interview that elicits information on a given issue from a carefully selected group of individuals (Grudens-Schuck, Allen, and Larson 2004). Focus groups are carefully planned and implemented by a trained moderator, whose task is to lead participants through a series of key questions and prompt for specific experiences and descriptions. Moderators also must take care to develop a nonthreatening environment to encourage all participants to share their points of view (Krueger and Casey 2009). Participants in focus groups are intentionally selected and typically have a common characteristic that unites them (e.g., language proficiency level, class year, enrollment in a specific course or university). Unlike a discussion, the goal of a focus group is to gather diverse perspectives rather than make a decision or build a consensus on a particular issue. As table 6.1 indicates, focus groups are distinguished from other kinds of discussion groups by several key features.

Table 6.1 A comparison of focus groups and discussion groups

Features	Focus groups	Discussion groups
Clear plan/focus	+	+/–
Moderator always present	+	–
Data collection is critical	+	–
Participants have common characteristics	+	+/–
Participants can argue different opinions	–	+
Builds consensus among participants	–	+
Purpose is to elicit perceptions and opinions	+	–

Note: "+" indicates presence of this feature, and "–" indicates absence of this feature.

Focus groups are always guided by a clear, specific plan, whereas discussion groups might be unstructured. Focus groups always include a moderator, whose job is to execute the plan, while discussion groups typically do not have a designated moderator. In focus groups, data collection by means of notes or recordings is critical for subsequent use in the evaluation, whereas in discussion groups data collection is not a critical component. Additionally, the overall purpose of a focus group is to elicit perceptions, opinions, previous experiences, and other reflections. Discussion groups are typically solution- or outcome-focused, and participants are able to argue with each other for their opinions. Focus groups differ in that participants may agree or disagree with each other, but there is no need to agree on a final outcome. The most important outcome in a focus group is the sharing of experiences.

When to Select a Focus Group

There are many reasons to use focus groups for an evaluation. However, focus-group data are not without limitations (see Marczak and Sewell 1991). The following section will help evaluators decide if a focus group is the right choice for data collection.

Advantages of Focus Groups

Focus groups have the advantage of being highly flexible. As with interviews, data collection can be adapted to a wide range of evaluation uses, stakeholders, and settings. Few resources other than a trained moderator and a recording device are necessary, making this a low-cost option when time and resources are tight. Focus groups collect qualitative information about the beliefs, attitudes, opinions, and perceptions of groups of people. Focus-group data, then, can help answer questions like: *Why* do participants feel the way they do? *How* can the program be improved? *How* should the new program be designed and implemented? Focus-group data thus enable evaluators to elicit ideas from key stakeholders and gather specific information on why those ideas are important.

Focus groups are distinct from the other forms of data collection described in this guide in several ways. A key difference with focus-group data collection, unlike interviews and questionnaires, is that participants are able to hear the ideas of the other focus-group members. This interaction between focus-group participants has the potential to trigger new ideas that participants may not have otherwise thought of on their own. This unique feature of focus groups is especially useful when evaluation calls for generating new information on, say, student needs or solutions to particular problems. In addition, the focus-group moderator is able to ask follow-up questions, probe participants to provide additional detail, and clarify or confirm their understanding. Unlike responses to selected-response items on questionnaires (multiple-choice items, rating scales, etc.), focus-group data are qualitative and descriptive in nature, which is advantageous for exploring or better understanding complex program processes, or, when working with stakeholders who dislike the kinds of statistical outputs questionnaire data commonly provide. Similar to questionnaire data, focus groups have the advantage of gathering information from multiple participants at once, which can save time and is more cost effective than interviewing stakeholders individually.

Disadvantages of Focus Groups
Focus groups also have a number of disadvantages evaluators must take into consideration. First, since focus-group data are collected in groups, the views of individuals within the focus group must be regarded as co-constructed and influenced by the other participants. Furthermore, focus-group data are cross-sectional, meaning they represent only a snapshot of a program at the time of data collection. For this reason, it is difficult to use focus groups as a means of longitudinal data collection to measure changes in perceptions or opinions over time. In addition, focus-group data are less amenable to quantification or statistical analysis and therefore should not be used when an evaluation needs data to support generalizations to larger populations (the goal of inferential statistical analyses). A related issue is that if focus groups are comprised of volunteers (of teachers, say), as they often are, the views captured during the session cannot not be regarded as representing the views of a wider group of similar respondents.

While the interactive nature of focus groups produces a uniquely useful data set, it can sometimes be difficult for the moderator to control and redirect participants to discuss the topics of interest. Off-topic discussion is more easily mitigated by the one-on-one nature of face-to-face interviews and is avoided altogether by questionnaires. For these reasons, moderators must be carefully trained to keep participants on track and to do so without biasing data-collection efforts. Similarly, focus groups are not well suited to gathering information on sensitive or face-threatening topics, since anonymity or confidentiality of responses cannot be guaranteed.[1]

Conducting a Focus Group
After careful consideration of the evaluation questions, uses, indicators, and other factors (resources, stakeholder needs, etc.), focus groups can be an excellent way to collect detailed, easy-to-understand data. Very often, stakeholders will want to understand complex processes within programs and why things are happening the way they are. Focus groups are well suited to providing this type of information. To these ends, the steps presented next will allow any evaluator or evaluation team to take advantage of the unique contributions of focus-group data while avoiding some of the pitfalls discussed above.

Stage 1: Planning a Focus Group

The first step in focus-group data collection is thoughtful alignment with the evaluation questions, uses, and indicators under investigation. Evaluators must ask themselves, "How will a focus group meet the needs of the evaluation users?" and "Which indicators does this type of data collection support best?"

Once the advantages and disadvantages of other types of data collection have been carefully weighed, the next step is to decide how to sample the relevant population necessary to answer evaluation questions and enable evaluation uses. Who are the specific stakeholders or informants who can provide the necessary information? Keep in mind that the group invited should share some unifying characteristic rather than representing a diverse pool. This way, participants will be less inclined to shy away from sharing their opinions in order to avoid conflict. Another sampling consideration has to do with cultural issues of status or age (important in many non-Western cultures), which may impact how some members interact with one another.

While there is no standard number of participants, a good rule of thumb is to invite double the number of participants desired (to compensate for absences), aiming for six to twelve attendees in total (Bader and Rossi 2002). A group of six to twelve ensures that each participant's voice can be heard without the group becoming too unwieldy. As always, consider the uses of the evaluation when selecting a representative group of participants and how users will regard the trustworthiness or appropriateness of responses of the particular individuals involved.

Next, the focus-group protocol that the moderator will follow during the session should be designed and aligned with the indicators of the evaluation. A focus-group protocol is a document that provides a set of guidelines on ways to consistently navigate the before, during, and after stages of focus-group administration. The questions or prompts from the protocol will center on five or six logically ordered key questions. All questions should be open-ended (avoid yes/no questions, such as "Do you like the language class?"). To start, opening and introductory questions can ask about participants' background information, break the ice, and allow them to become comfortable in the focus group. A transition question helps participants begin to focus on the topic that will motivate the key questions to follow. Always include a concluding question to ask participants if there was anything else they should have discussed or wanted to discuss that was not covered (see table 6.2 for an example of a focus-group protocol).

Finally, it is highly recommended to pilot (i.e., try out) the focus-group protocol before actually sitting down with focus-group participants. Piloting will provide valuable feedback on the types of data the focus-group questions will obtain. For example, the wording of key questions might not elicit the extent of responses expected, resulting in a focus group that provides insufficient data to shed light on evaluation questions. On the other hand, a question might elicit unrelated responses that waste valuable time and produce unhelpful data. Practicing the questions, instructions, and other procedures will provide an estimate of how long the focus group will last, an invaluable piece of logistical information. Piloting is also useful training for the moderator (or useful practice if the moderator is also the evaluator or researcher). The moderator should be ready to prioritize key information, probe where necessary, and keep participants on track. The moderator should also not be a supervisor or at a higher professional rank than the focus-group participants.

● Table 6.2 Example focus-group protocol

Question type	Example
Opening	Tell us your name and how long you have been a part of the program.
Introductory	How was it that you first learned about the program?
Transition	Think back to when you first became involved in the program. What were your first impressions?
Key(s)	How do you feel that your language background is being supported in the program?
Ending	Is there anything we should have talked about but didn't?

Stage 2: Moderating a Focus Group

Once the protocol is piloted and the participants are invited, the room should be prepared for the focus-group session. Before participants arrive, the moderator should set up chairs or tables so that participants are sitting in a circle and can easily see one another. Special care should be taken while setting up the recording device so that all voices are within range and without the device being too conspicuously apparent. Multiple recording devices are recommended in the event that one fails, and each should be tested prior to the start of the focus-group session. If resources allow, one or more notetakers should also be present to manually record data, which will aid in subsequent analysis and transcriptions (and also serves as a backup should recording devices fail).

Once the participants have arrived, the moderator should introduce herself/himself, thank the attendees for their participation, and explain the purpose of the focus group clearly and concisely. This is also the time when the moderator should obtain informed consent from the participants to be recorded and provide information about privacy, confidentiality, and use of participant responses, if applicable (see chapter 5). These steps are key to establishing the nonthreatening environment necessary for successful data collection. In addition, since it is likely that some attendees have never participated in a focus group before, it is important to inform participants about the nature of a focus group and how it differs from a discussion. Let participants know they do not need to agree, but they do need to be respectful of each other's opinions and allow everyone to speak one at a time. Finally, allow time for participants to ask any questions about their rights as participants in the data collection, the evaluation project, and about how the focus group will be conducted.

During the question period, the moderator should be aware of several aspects of the focus-group interaction. Primarily, the moderator should probe participants for additional detail on the topics under discussion, asking questions, such as the following:

- "Could you give an example?"
- "Can you talk more about that?"
- "Could you say why you feel that way?"

Asking these types of questions enables the moderator to obtain sufficient detail about the focus-group questions. The moderator should also take care to avoid reacting positively or negatively to participants' answers, remaining respectfully neutral so as to avoid biasing informants' responses (and evaluation results). An additional aim should be to allow for natural conversation to develop between participants rather than questioning participants one at a time, person by person. However, if participants are hesitant to talk at first, ask someone to begin. Furthermore, if conversation slows before a key question has been sufficiently addressed, to move along the conversation, ask the following:

- "Does anyone else have a similar or different perspective?"
- "Can anyone add to that idea?"
- "Has anyone had a different experience?"

If participants have over-addressed a particular question, the moderator should intervene and move participants on to the next topic. If off-topic conversation needs to be halted, the moderator can say something like:

- "Let's return to our discussion on [key question topic]."
- "Does anyone have a different perspective on [restate key question]?"

Perhaps the most important responsibility of the moderator is to ensure that everyone has an opportunity to speak and no one person is dominating the group. The moderator might encourage a shy participant to speak, for example, by simply asking, "What is your perspective?" At the end of the focus group, be sure to thank the participants, ask if there are any topics that were not addressed, and provide contact information should participants wish to contact you with any follow-up concerns or questions.

Stage 3: Analyzing Focus-Group Data

There are many ways in which focus-group data can be analyzed (see chapter 9 for one approach). The direction to take in the analysis depends on the evaluation uses, questions, and indicators as well as the resources available to the evaluation team. Transcriptions of the audio recordings can make for easy analysis but are costly and time-consuming to produce. When time or funding is scarce, important ideas and concepts can be taken from the focus-group notes and supplemented with key quotes from the audio recordings. (Tip: Ask notetakers to record time stamps during the focus group for particularly valuable quotes or simply for each key question to make the audio recordings easier to navigate.) A thematic analysis of key concepts is often a useful strategy when working with focus-group data and qualitative data in general (see Miles, Huberman, and Saldaña 2014), carefully noting both what participants said, as well as what topics were avoided.

Regardless of the method of analysis chosen, the data obtained from a focus group can be utilized to develop other data-collection techniques and narrow evaluation foci. Depending on the needs of the evaluation, the data from a focus group may inform questionnaire development. Alternatively, the results from a questionnaire might be supplemented with qualitative data from a follow-up focus group. In either case, evaluations can often require multiple focus groups with multiple sets of stakeholder groups. If so, it will be clear when sufficient numbers of focus groups have been conducted when the information elicited starts to repeat that from previous focus groups.

Using Focus Groups for Language Program Evaluations

As previously described, focus groups are able to collect robust qualitative data for a variety of evaluation purposes. While focus groups are popularly utilized in marketing research, they have also been profitably implemented in language program evaluations and educational research (e.g., Lynch 2000). When conducting focus groups to inform language program evaluation, there are a few additional recommendations to keep in mind.

When conducting evaluations in the language education domain, it may be that the evaluation team will be working with multilingual participants, which will require a translator. Multilingual participants may wish to express themselves in any of their languages or may wish to switch between them. In order to have this option available, train a moderator who is also proficient in the languages of the participants. If focus-group data are translated, "back-translate" the data with a second translator back into the original language and check to make sure the two translations convey similar ideas; this will uncover any translation errors or flawed or inaccurate interpretations made on the part of the first translator. Additionally, be sure to indicate in the data which language participants decided to use at various points in the focus-group conversation. The particular language used at key points in the session could have a bearing on the evaluation findings.

Finally, many language program evaluations include hierarchies of stakeholders, such as students, their teachers, and administrators. Focus groups should never mix participants at different organizational levels, as this will affect how comfortable they are in responding to questions, thereby threatening the trustworthiness of the results. Clear explanations of confidentiality and respondent privacy are of the utmost importance in this evaluation scenario as well.

Focus groups can produce high-quality data for an evaluation if utilized for the right evaluative purposes and if implemented effectively. Systematic analysis of focus-group results can provide information that other data-collection strategies might miss or are unable to account for. Given the many advantages of focus groups, evaluators of language programs or language educators should consider integrating this method of data collection into their future evaluations—provided, of course, that focus groups will offer information about user-selected indicators that can inform user-generated evaluation questions.[2]

Scenarios: Example Focus-Group Protocols

In scenario 1, evaluation question 2 seeks to identify the changes or innovations that are needed to better support lab users and campus stakeholders. One indicator for this evaluation question is the desired uses of the language lab by users, staff, and campus stakeholders. A focus group would be well suited to address this indicator by targeting specific stakeholder populations; this way, evaluators can readily compare and contrast the diverse needs of the language-lab users by holding multiple iterations of focus groups. Table 6.3 provides a sample focus-group protocol for addressing the needs of the heritage language learner population in this scenario.

In scenario 2, evaluation question 1 seeks to identify the language-learning needs of the English language learners at the center. One indicator that addresses this question asks, "What can program alumni do and not do in English in professional and education contexts?" A focus group, when conducted in the participants' native language, is well equipped to address this indicator. The second example protocol in table 6.3 is targeted at a group of alumni who are all working in similar fields (e.g., service industries). A focus group enables evaluators to gather domain-specific needs of key stakeholder groups quickly and efficiently.

Scenario 3's evaluation question 1 asks how satisfied students and teachers are with the Chinese telecollaboration program. Focus groups targeting specific stakeholder groups can address several indicators at once to answer this evaluation question. The third example protocol in table 6.3 is designed for a group of students who participated in the program and addresses indicators of satisfaction, usefulness, and motivation both during the telecollaboration sessions and to pursue Chinese in the future. A focus group will use the social nature of this group of key stakeholders to generate ideas. However, a focus group with a group of high-school students will necessarily need to be adapted to meet the needs of this population. Ground rules should be explicit and teachers or administrators should not be present to avoid biasing student responses.

Notes

1. Evaluators should give assurances about privacy and confidentiality of responses and request that participants not discuss any topics outside of the focus group. However, it is best practice to caution that there is no guarantee views expressed within the focus group will not be shared outside the session by other participants.
2. For additional advice on conducting focus groups see Fern (2001); Grudens-Schuck, Allen, and Larson (2004); and Krueger and Casey (2009).

Table 6.3 Scenarios: Example focus-group protocols

Scenario 1	Question type	Example
Community College Language Lab	Opening	Tell us your name and how long you have been a student at the community college.
	Introductory	How was it that you first came to visit the language lab?
	Transition	Think back to when you first visited the language lab. What were your first impressions?
	Key(s)	How useful are the current lab resources for your learning needs?
		How is the language lab meeting the needs of heritage language learners in particular?
		What changes could be made to the language lab to better meet your language-learning needs?
		What kinds of lab equipment or technology would you like to see in the language lab?
	Ending	Are there any aspects of the language lab you wanted to discuss that we didn't cover?
Scenario 2	**Question type**	**Example**
Adult Language Program Needs Analysis	Opening	Tell us your name and what profession you are currently working in.
	Introductory	When and for how long were you a student at the language program?
	Transition	Think back to when you first left the language program. How confident did you feel in your language abilities?
	Key(s)	What kinds of activities are easy for you to accomplish in English at your profession?
		What kinds of activities are difficult for you to accomplish in English at your profession?
		How could the adult ESL program have better prepared you to be successful in your current profession?
	Ending	Are there any aspects of your language needs that you wanted to discuss that we didn't cover?

(continued)

● Table 6.3 *Scenarios: Example focus-group protocols (continued)*

Scenario 3	Question type	Example
Eleventh-grade Chinese Telecollaboration	Opening	Tell us your name and your favorite subject in school.
	Introductory	Why did you decide to start studying Chinese?
	Transition	Think back to the first time you Skyped with the students in China. What were you thinking at the time?
	Key(s)	Describe what class is like when you are preparing to talk with your language partners and also when you are chatting with your language partners on Skype.
		Tell us what you like most about talking with your language partners in China.
		Tell us what you dislike about talking with your language partners in China.
		Has talking with language partners motivated you to continue to study Chinese? Why or why not?
	Ending	Are there any parts of the Chinese program that we should have talked about but didn't get a chance to?

7

Conducting Evaluation Interviews

JORGE MÉNDEZ SEIJAS, JANIRE ZALBIDEA, and CRISTI VALLEJOS

THE NUMBER OF INTERVIEWS that take place in the media and in other areas of our lives may give the impression that interviews are straightforward and easy to conduct (Patton 2015). While interviews may appear similar to natural conversation, they must be carefully planned and implemented so that the information they elicit is useful for evaluation purposes. To help evaluators conduct productive evaluation interviews, this chapter provides guidelines for (1) identifying when interviews are an appropriate data-collection tool; (2) distinguishing among the different types of interviews available for evaluation purposes; and (3) planning, designing, and conducting a successful interview.

Evaluation Interviews

Interviews are an effective tool for evaluation since they collect information on the perspectives of those most knowledgeable about the program—staff, students, and other invested stakeholders. Interviews can be defined broadly as a type of conversation (Kvale 1996), though one that is purposeful and has the particular aim of collecting information relevant for a program evaluation project. The purpose of conducting interviews is to have individuals report on their beliefs, opinions, abilities, and perceptions of the educational processes happening within their program (Kvale 1996; Patton 1990). To these ends, the interviewer must play the role of attentive listener (rather than equal participant) and draw out honest, unbiased, thoughtful responses from the interviewee on a particular topic.

To be effective, an evaluation interview must be planned and organized in a systematic way. An important aspect of evaluation interviews, then, is that they must collect information on project indicators (see chapter 4). Again, the purpose of identifying indicators prior to data collection is to specify and clarify the particular types of evidence relevant for answering evaluation questions and facilitating evaluation uses. Creating interview questions that are unrelated to evaluation indicators (and questions and uses) risks collecting information unrelated to evaluation aims.

When to Use an Interview

Interviews are similar to focus groups in that respondents give their views via spoken comments. Like focus groups, the interviewer can probe the interviewee for additional information, ask clarification questions, and explore particular ideas, all of which leads to greater and richer detail in the interviewee's responses. In this way, interviews provide an opportunity to explore complex educational processes from the point of view of a program insider. Interviews, then, are effective for exploring *why* and *how* things are happening in a program, which can be useful when stakeholders want to identify instructors' or students' teaching or learning needs, or better understand why particular aspects of the program are "effective" or "useful," or—when a program is not functioning as expected—identify what should be done to change and improve it. When an evaluation project calls for these types of complex issues to be explored in depth, interviews can be an effective data-collection option.

Of course, interviews differ from focus groups in important ways, which may lead to choosing one tool over the other. As noted in chapter 6, information collected from focus-groups comes from discussions between multiple participants and is the by-product of group dynamics. Interviews, by contrast, are one-on-one interactions, with just the interviewer and interviewee participating in the conversation. As such, interviews may offer more privacy so that informants can speak more openly and honestly about their opinions. A more private set of circumstances may be desirable when participants are prompted to speak on sensitive topics. Relatedly, interviews may suit shy individuals or informants otherwise reluctant to share their views in front of other people.

In addition, interviews can be an effective (and sometimes the only) way to collect the views of particular individuals. For example, interviews can be useful with expert informants better able to elaborate on program processes within a one-on-one scenario. People in positions of leadership are also good targets for an interview. Managers and supervisors often have particularly well-informed views, though such individuals may be few in number and may not have sufficiently flexible schedules to participate in a focus group. When particular individuals have specialized knowledge and especially valuable views to impart, the one-on-one aspect of interviews lends itself well to collecting information from these informants.

These advantages notwithstanding, certain practical considerations should be borne in mind when considering interviews for data collection. Carrying out interviews requires a nontrivial amount of time, effort, and human resources compared to questionnaires or focus groups. Since interviews collect data from one person at a time, they involve scheduling logistics and travel considerations. In addition, the comments-type data interviews commonly produce can be time-consuming to transcribe and analyze.

Another evaluation-related use (and benefit) of interviews is to supplement other data-collection methods. For example, interviews—like focus groups—can be used in questionnaire development. At the start of an evaluation project, interviews can identify issues or topics of interest (e.g., strengths and weakness of a new approach to instruction, student learning needs, best teaching practices), which can then be transferred into a questionnaire and administered to a larger population of informants. Interviews can also be used after a questionnaire has been administered (see chapter 8); evaluators can use interviews to follow up with respondents, asking them to expand and elaborate on their questionnaire responses. This type of follow-up can be an effective way to iteratively explore and further understand program elements.

Types of Interviews for Program Evaluation

Several different types of evaluation interviews are available to evaluators, each with advantages and disadvantages for evaluation purposes. Patton (2015) provides a classification of different types of evaluation interviews in terms of their structuredness, or how much freedom and flexibility they allow for probing, follow-up questions, and interviewer involvement. The types include (1) the interview guide approach, (2) standardized open-ended interviews, and (3) closed-field response interviews.[1]

In the interview guide approach, the interviewer comes with a predetermined set of topics or questions, though the interviewer has the freedom to ask about other topics while the interview is happening. Set topics give the interview structure and prompt interviewees to speak on issues directly related to project indicators, but the interviewer can also formulate questions during the interview to probe relevant issues. The semi-structured nature of the interview guide approach allows for the collection of information on similar themes from different respondents, but also allows for exploring in novel directions, which can generate new, interesting ideas relevant to evaluation aims. A disadvantage of the interview guide approach, however, is the risk that with more freedom to ask unprepared questions, informants' responses may not always relate directly to project indicators.

Standardized open-ended interviews involve asking interviewees a carefully designed, predetermined set of questions. The interview is standardized by developing an "interview protocol," a document that specifies the steps, materials, equipment, pre-interview dialogues, questions, probes, and participants involved in the interview (see figure 7.1). The protocol assists with standardization by ensuring that the interview is conducted in exactly the same way on each occasion by a single interviewer or by different interviewers. Standardized open-ended interviews offer certain advantages for program evaluation. Using exactly the same questions for all participants enhances comparability of information between respondents. In addition, the information gathered from interviewees will more likely be directly related to project indicators. And interviewer bias is reduced since interviewers stick to preset procedures, questions, and probes.

Lastly, a closed-field response interview involves asking preset questions but also providing interviewees with a selection of possible answers to choose from (which are read to the interviewee). Closed-field response interviews are akin to a spoken questionnaire. Information provided from this type of interview (yes/no responses, extent of agreement responses, multiple-choice responses, etc.) can be collected, recorded, and analyzed relatively easily and quickly using quantitative or statistical analysis. Closed-field response interviews are similar to questionnaires in that they are useful for finding out what program informants think about known issues or program elements as well as what proportions of respondents share similar views (see chapter 8). This method, however, prevents the interviewer from learning something about the program, or what respondents think, beyond what is addressed in the interview questions themselves.

Patton's interview strategies are one way of distinguishing between different approaches to conducting interviews for evaluation purposes. Each offers different benefits and advantages, though evaluators should feel free to use, modify, or combine any of the above approaches as they see fit. Ultimately, the choice of how to conduct an interview should be based on the approach that will enable evaluation users to use the evaluation in the ways they desire.

Planning, Designing, and Conducting an Effective Interview

Standardized open-ended interviews and the interview guide approach are arguably the most common types of interview for program evaluation. Thus, the remainder of this chapter will largely focus on developing materials for these two interview types. The next sections discuss key aspects of planning, designing, and conducting evaluation interviews.

Planning for an Evaluation Interview

Conducting an effective interview requires having a well-organized plan. As with focus groups (and questionnaires), the first step in interview planning should be a careful consideration of the project indicators. When writing interview prompts or questions, each item should have a direct link to one or more project indicators. It is the evaluator's responsibility to ensure that this is the case.

Next, interview prompts or questions should ideally be listed in an interview protocol, which describes the interview session in detail. Again, an interview protocol (like a focus-group protocol) is a document that lays out the procedures, participants, equipment, materials, prompts or questions, probes, and timing of the interview session. An example protocol is shown in figure 7.1.

Creating an effective interview protocol and conducting an effective interview session require consideration of four key design factors: (1) writing high-quality questions; (2) sequencing questions in helpful ways; (3) piloting the protocol; and (4) conducting the interview systematically so that respondents provide detailed, complete, honest, and unbiased information.

Designing an Effective Interview: Writing Questions

The specific wording of interview questions is crucial to collecting useful interview information. To this end, interview questions should be (1) open-ended, (2) clear, (3) neutral (unbiased), and (4) ask about a single issue.

Ensuring an item is open-ended means it is possible for interviewees to give comprehensive answers, including any details they deem appropriate. For example, a question such as, "How well do the students in the program attain course learning outcomes?" may at first glance appear open-ended. A response to this question, however, could be "very well," or "poorly," or a similar response to an equally limited set of possible response options. Changing the wording could elicit more extensive responses: "What do you think about students' abilities to reach course learning outcomes?" This question is now more open-ended because the interviewee is asked to express their thoughts and perspectives more generally about student performance in relation to the student learning outcomes.

In addition to being open-ended, questions must also be clear so that the interviewee can understand what they are being asked. This is a particular concern for multilingual speakers who may be using a second language to provide responses. For such participants, prompts must use simple sentence structures, nontechnical language, and high-frequency vocabulary.

Questions must also be neutral or unbiased. Bias refers to influencing responses by how questions are worded or sequenced, or, by the manner in which they are asked. Precautions should be taken to ensure that interview questions do not influence the interviewee in a way that leads to an untruthful or otherwise altered response. For example, a question such as "How easy is it to use the language lab resources provided by the program?" is biased because it presupposes that the language lab is easy to use in the first place and may prevent a critical response. The bias in this question can be reduced by asking about aspects of the lab that are both difficult and easy to use: "What aspects of the language lab resources do you find easy to use?" and "What aspects of the language lab resources do you find difficult to use?"

Finally, items should not be "double-barreled"—that is, asking two questions in a single prompt and therefore requiring two answers. For example, a question such as, "Do you make use of the resources provided in the language lab? Why or why not?" the interviewee is expected to answer two questions at once and may not provide as complete an answer as is expected. Revising the question as follows can help remedy its double-barreled structure: "The community college provides a language lab with various resources to students enrolled in language courses. What has been your experience with the lab?" The revised version asks for a response on a single issue rather than two.

Designing an Effective Interview: Sequencing Questions

Although there are no fixed rules as to how questions must be sequenced, it is recommended that prompts be grouped by topic. In addition, within each topic, the simpler question should be presented first, followed by more complex questions. Furthermore, the most important questions should appear relatively early in the interview, and sensitive questions should be left toward the end of the interview once rapport has been established.

Designing an Effective Interview: Piloting

Once the interview protocol is created, a number of strategies should be used to ensure the protocol is effective and functioning as intended. First, the protocol and items should be reviewed by experienced colleagues or people knowledgeable about interview data-collection methods. Next, the protocol should be piloted (i.e., practiced or tested) with respondents similar to those who will eventually participate in the interview sessions. The purpose of piloting is to test if instructions are clear, if the items are eliciting the desired information, and if the behavior of interviewers is appropriate and not biasing informant responses. To this end, it is also helpful to have an experienced colleague observe the pilot interview session and provide feedback. Evaluators can also ask the pilot interviewees follow-up questions about whether the prompts or instructions were unclear or confusing.

Conducting an Effective Interview

When conducting the interview, the interviewer must keep in mind two responsibilities: first, they must establish rapport with the participants so that they feel comfortable and willing to provide detailed, thoughtful information, and second, they must maintain control over the interaction so that the respondent provides relevant information.

To build rapport, interviewers need to be "good listeners" and show that they genuinely care about what the interviewees are saying. To do so, interviewers should first explain the rationale for why they are asking the particular interview questions; this helps participants understand the questions while feeling valued as an important source and supplier of program information. In addition, nodding, periodically taking notes, and acknowledging the interviewee's points by saying "uh-huh" from time to time sends a message that the interviewer is actively listening and interested in the interviewee's views.

Note also that interviewers should avoid acting in a way that biases informant responses. For example, showing excessive agreement, interest, or sympathy with the respondents' answers—or, conversely, showing subtle disapproval, disagreement, a lack of interest—can alter how respondents will respond to subsequent questions. Feedback during interviews should be as neutral as possible.

To maintain control of the interview, interviewers must be aware of the evaluation goals in terms of the project indicators and evaluation questions. If interviewees get off track, the interviewer must respectfully interject and redirect the discussion back to relevant topics. If the digression resulted from a misinterpretation, the interviewer should quickly rephrase the question. The interviewer can also establish ground rules at the beginning of the interview, making it clear that the interviewee will be interrupted if responses are unrelated to the interview question. Lastly, if responses are excessively terse and uninformative, interviewers must probe as necessary to elicit relevant information (e.g., "Could you talk more about that?").

Interviews in Language Program Evaluation

It will often be the case in language program evaluation that interviews will involve multilingual participants whose language is different from the one being used for the evaluation. Such participants raise a number of issues unique to language program evaluation.

In instances where respondents do not speak the same language as the evaluators, interpreters may be needed to participate in interview sessions to either interpret or to take on the role of interviewer. As noted in chapter 6, regardless of whether a nonnative or native-speaking interviewer is used, the person should be trained in effective interviewing techniques (noting some of the advice above) and should definitely participate in piloting sessions to ensure that they understand how to conduct the interview.

Relatedly, if the protocol has been translated into another language—for example, from English to Spanish—a back-translating strategy can be used to ensure that the translated Spanish questions are still expressing the meaning of the original items written in English. Back-translation involves using a different translator to translate the items in the Spanish-language protocol back into English and a comparison of the translated items with the original English items to check that the meaning of the items has not changed in the translation process (as noted in chapter 6, back-translating can also be used for data analysis).

For multilingual speakers—particularly those for whom the language of the interview interaction is a second language—reporting on these individuals' responses presents certain issues and considerations of privacy and confidentiality. Often, evaluators will want to quote a notable response from an interviewee in a report. Note that doing so can identify nonnative users of a language, particularly if there are a small number of nonnative speakers in the respondent population. Extreme caution is needed when quoting multilingual speakers in ways that may identify them; their responses may need to be omitted from reporting in order to protect their privacy.

Finally, in addition to the language-related issues noted above, there may be cases when instructors might be willing to act as interviewers to gather information from their students. Although familiarity between the interviewer and the interviewee offers advantages in building rapport, instructor-student interviews introduce dynamics that are likely to result in students not sharing fully honest views. Such arrangements are to be avoided.

Scenarios: Example Interview Protocols

In the remainder of the chapter we provide example interview protocols for each of the volume scenarios (see table 7.1).[2] In scenario 1, evaluation question 1 seeks to address the degree to which the language lab is supporting language education. In this instance, interviews would be useful with a small number of stakeholders, such as instructors and students, to determine items that could be used on a later questionnaire to be distributed to all language students. Specifically, information obtained from interviews targeting indicators 3–8 (frequent uses of the lab, frequently used equipment, usefulness of resources, satisfaction with resources, and deterrents to lab use) could be employed to design questionnaire items that ask participants to rate perceived usefulness of or satisfaction with program features. In scenario 2, the goal of evaluation question 1 is to assess the needs of students in the program. The indicator to address this question is "felt language-learning needs by the students." In this instance, because the goal is to elicit the opinions of students who may have limited writing ability in English, a structured interview can best assist in gathering this information. The students may also feel more comfortable expressing this information in an interview as opposed to a focus group because it provides more confidentiality.

For scenario 3, an interview with the telecollaboration instructors would be a fruitful, informative method to shed light on the "usefulness of the telecollaboration program for student learning" as well as "student motivation and engagement during telecollaboration sessions." Sample interview questions addressing these project indicators are listed in table 7.1 (again, see figure 7.1 for an example of a full interview protocol).

Notes

1. Patton includes a fourth type of interview, informal conversational interview, which we do not address here.
2. For additional resources on conducting interviews see Kvale (1996), Colker (N.d.) and Patton (2015).

Scenario 1: Community College Language Lab

Instructions	Thank you for agreeing to participate in this interview. The total time for this interview should be no more than thirty minutes. Be aware that since our time is limited I may need to interrupt you and bring us back on topic in order to finish the interview on time.
	Do you have any questions before we begin?
	To start, I am going to ask you some questions about your use of the language lab.
Warm-up	1. What language are you studying currently?
Prompts	2. On average, how many times do you use the language lab per week?
	3. What activities do you use the language lab for?
	4. What equipment in the language lab do you use?
	5. What factors stop you from using the lab?
	6. What aspects of the resources provided do you find easy to use?
	7. What aspects of the resources provided do you find difficult to use?
	8. How would you describe your experiences using the lab?
	9. What experience with computer labs did you have before coming to Maguire Community College?
	10. What suggestions do you have for improving lab spaces?
Final prompt	11. Is there anything else you would like to tell me about your experiences with the lab?
Closing	Thank you very much for your time and thoughts. If you have anything you'd like to add to your responses, please feel free to contact me.

Scenario 2: Adult Language Program Needs Analysis

Instructions	Thank you for participating in this interview. I am going to ask you some questions about what you need English for in your life. If at any time you don't understand what I am saying, please let me know.
	Do you have any questions before we begin?
	Okay, let's start.
Warm-up	1. How long have you been taking English classes?
Prompts	2. When do you use English most frequently?
	3. When do you feel that using English is most difficult?
	4. How has the English class improved your English?
	5. What do you still need to get better at in English?
	6. What are your future English learning goals?
	7. What could the school do to make the ESL classes better?
Final prompt	8. Is there anything else you would like to tell me before we finish?
Closing	Thank you very much for your time. If you want to tell more, please feel free to contact me.

Scenario 3: Eleventh-grade Chinese Telecollaboration

Instructions	As noted in my invitation email, we are interviewing the Chinese telecollaboration instructors about their experiences teaching the program.
	Note that since we are limited for time and have a number of items to get through, I may need to interrupt you and move on to a different question.
	Do you understand the instructions? Do you have any questions before we begin?
	Okay, let's get started.
Warm-Up	1. Can you tell me a bit about how the telecollaboration course got started?

(continued)

● **Table 7.1** Scenarios: Example interview prompts (*continued*)

Prompts	2. What did you think about facilitating the telecollaboration sessions?
	3. How are the telecollaboration activities designed to make learning happen?
	4. What aspects of telecollaboration do you think have been most helpful for student learning?
	5. What aspects of telecollaboration have been challenging for students?
	6. How motivated or engaged did students appear to be during the telecollaboration sessions?
	7. At what times were they most engaged or motivated?
	8. At what times were they least engaged or motivated?
	9. What suggestions do you have for improving the telecollaboration course?
	10. Do you think the telecollaboration course should be continued?
Final Prompt	11. Is there anything else you'd like to tell me about the Chinese telecollaboration course?
Closing	Thank you very much for your time and thoughts. If you have anything you'd like to add to your responses, please feel free to contact me.

"Defining student learning outcomes for the Maguire Community College Spanish language program"

1. Purpose of the interview

   The purpose of the interview is to elicit from Maguire Community College (MCC) Spanish language instructors the key student learning outcomes (SLOs) for Spanish students completing two years of study at MCC. The information from participants will help the Spanish program assessment committee create SLO statements that describe the specific skills, understandings, and dispositions that students should have attained at the end of the program.

2. Timing and location

   - Time: Approximately 30–45 minutes
   - Location: Somewhere convenient for the participants (office, cafeteria, classroom, etc.)

3. Participants

   - Interviewer
   - Notetaker
   - Interviewee/Course instructor

4. Materials/Equipment

   - Copy of protocol
   - Digital audio recorder
   - Consent form (for the interviewee)
   - Copy of interview questions (for the interviewee)

5. Pre-interview procedures

   Participants receive an email prior to the interview listing the following:

   - Consent form
   - Interview questions
   - A general reminder to review their course syllabi to inform responses

6. Interview procedures

   Opening:

   - Evaluator/Interviewer brief self-introduction
   - Interviewer explains who they are/their role in the evaluation project

   Describe the purpose of the interview:

   "The purpose of this interview is to discuss your opinions about important student learning expectations for MCC Spanish-degree graduates. The reason I am collecting this information is because the MCC Spanish assessment committee

(continued)

wants to develop and clearly define student learning outcomes for MCC Spanish students. In order to do so, the MCC assessment committee is interested in faculty views on what some of these learning targets could be. The information we collect from you and other faculty will be used to develop consensus on the specific statements of skills, knowledge, and dispositions for Spanish study at MCC."

Explain the procedure:

● Briefly review content of the consent form.
● Ask participant to read and sign the form.
● Ask if there are any questions.

"Let's begin. As stated, we will be taking notes, but if it's okay with you, we would like to record the discussion so that we do not miss anything you have to say. As you know, everything you say will be confidential. The interview will last approximately thirty to forty-five minutes. If there are any questions that you would prefer not to answer, please let me know and we can move on."

Interview questions/Prompts

1. In your opinion, what are the most important Spanish language abilities that students should master upon graduating from MCC?

   One way to answer this question is to finish or consider the following sentence: "Upon finishing their Spanish studies at MCC, students should be able to...[do what?]"

2. In terms of important *understanding* or *knowledge*, what should students have mastered upon graduating from MCC?

   Again, it might be helpful to answer this question by completing the following sentence: "Upon finishing their Spanish studies at MCC, students should know about or understand...[what?]"

3. What kinds of *dispositions* should we expect students to have developed? By dispositions, I mean attitudes, values, or ethics that characterize a multilingual speaker of Spanish from the MCC program.

4. Thinking now about the course(s) that you teach, what skills, understandings, or dispositions do students develop in your course?

5. What additional skills, understandings, or dispositions do you think would be beneficial for this course?

Closing

"Thank you for your cooperation. If you would like to add anything to your responses, please feel free to contact me and we can meet again, or you can send me your comments via email."

8

Questionnaires for Evaluation

AMY I. KIM and JOHN McE. DAVIS

QUESTIONNAIRES ARE A VERSATILE tool for use in program evaluation. They elicit information by having respondents choose answer options (e.g., multiple-choice questions or agreement ratings) or by supplying written or typed text (e.g., on items that ask for comments). Like focus groups and interviews, questionnaires are another way of collecting stakeholder views on the educational processes happening within their programs. Questionnaires can be used to obtain any of the types of information that people can supply about themselves or their environment, such as their perceptions, attitudes, feelings, opinions, preferences, behaviors, or perceived language abilities. Questionnaires are arguably the most commonly used evaluation tool, though they can be effective for certain evaluation-related aims and less effective for others. In this chapter, we address some key aspects of designing and administering questionnaires in order to provide useful information for language program evaluation.

Evaluation Questionnaires: Advantages

As noted throughout this guide, the instinctive and quick impulse to use questionnaires for program evaluation presents certain risks. Questionnaires are effective for providing certain types of information about a language program that may or may not be useful depending on stakeholders' and users' evaluation needs. The various ways in which questionnaires are helpful for evaluation projects can be divided into two broad categories: (1) the logistical advantages issuing from questionnaire administration, and (2) the advantages provided by questionnaire-type information.

Questionnaires are useful for evaluation purposes because of a number of administration or logistical advantages. A main advantage is their efficiency; questionnaires are quick to develop, easy to administer, cost-effective, and accessible from just about anywhere via mail or email. These advantages taken together lead to a main administration benefit: information can be collected from large numbers of respondents. If a project needs to capture the views of a large number of students, teachers, alumni, or parents, questionnaires will often be the best option to shed light on what a large group thinks about programmatic issues (and the best option to collect those views in a relatively short period of time).

A number of information-related advantages comes from the ability of questionnaires to reach large groups of evaluation informants. Historically, the main purpose of questionnaire research was to find out what a group of individuals thinks about a specific topic, garnering those views on the basis of a smaller sample of respondents (Dillman, Smyth, and Christian 2014). Likewise, evaluation purposes will often call for knowing whether certain known program elements are "useful" or "effective," ranking program elements for importance, indicating agreement with statements or assertions about the program, rating language abilities or attitudes about learning, and so on. As such, evaluation questionnaires can identify notable patterns of opinion in entire groups of program stakeholders. Moreover, if questionnaire administration is conducted carefully, results from questionnaires can be generalized to a population, which can be useful—or even necessary—for certain evaluations where it is important to know about majority views on important program issues. Doing so, however, requires a systematic approach to sampling (i.e., probability sampling) and high responses rates. Yet, if these things are done, questionnaires can collect large amounts of representative information that capture what a majority of stakeholders thinks about particular program elements.

Another important administration benefit of questionnaires is that data collection and analysis is quick and relatively efficient. Online questionnaire design and administration software, such as Google Forms, SurveyMonkey, and Qualtrics (among others), permits users to quickly download results in various file formats. Many online questionnaire platforms also allow users to automatically generate charts, figures, and other forms of data visualization that can be used to instantly analyze results.

An additional information-related advantage of questionnaires is that they provide numerical, quantitative data. Percentages or counts of yes/no or true/false responses; proportions of selected responses; and average ratings of usefulness, effectiveness, agreement, or language abilities are parsimonious, easy to interpret, and allow for statistical analysis (see chapter 9). In addition, quantitative results may satisfy particular users' data preferences (e.g., stakeholders who have a desire for "hard," statistical data), which may be needed for buy-in from key project stakeholders.

Finally, questionnaires have the ability to reduce certain types of response bias. Since questionnaires offer a certain amount of anonymity compared to interviews and focus groups, respondents are more likely to provide honest views and opinions. In addition, since there is no interviewer or focus-group facilitator involved in collecting responses, questionnaire results are free from the sorts of influence and bias that can arise from human interaction (though they are suspect to other kinds of bias from item wording or sequencing, as discussed below).

What Evaluation Questionnaires Can and Cannot Do

A key point to make about questionnaires is that they are useful for capturing information on *issues that are known and/or relatively well defined.* Accordingly, questionnaires have certain constraints that should be kept in mind. For example, all things being equal, questionnaire respondents will be more likely to complete selected-response items (e.g., multiple-choice questions, rating questions) than constructed, open-response items (i.e., typing or writing in comment boxes). Open-ended items are often left blank since they are more labor-intensive and time consuming to complete (issues that can be compounded by language proficiency). Therefore, questionnaires are best for capturing the static-type information contained in selected-response items. If evaluators or users want to use a questionnaire, they must have a good sense of the specific issues relevant to the evaluation project for which they need respondent feedback.

Questionnaires are less effective for exploring, developing, or generating issues of interest. For example, in a needs-analysis project, a focus group or interview would be better for brainstorming an initial list of student needs. Group dynamics, discussion, follow-up questioning, and probing make this kind of knowledge-generation possible. A questionnaire, by contrast, would not be as effective given the likelihood that respondents—unless very motivated—typically will not go to the trouble of writing extensive ideas about their needs in a comment box (especially if writing in second language). If a provisional list of needs was generated first via interviews or focus groups, those needs could then be listed in a questionnaire format and respondents could be asked to rate or rank them for importance, priority, or relevance. Questionnaires serve this latter function well, though again, a clear, prior sense of the project issues of interest is needed first.

Another issue to consider with questionnaires is how low response rates can impact the accuracy and trustworthiness of results. The questionnaire response rate is the number of people who completed the survey divided by the number of people who received the survey. A small proportion of responses can be regarded as unrepresentative of the views of the entire population (an issue known as "nonresponse error") and therefore perceived by users as untrustworthy. Note also that response rates for online or mailed questionnaires are rarely high. The impact or likelihood of a low response rate—and the fact that results may not represent the whole population—should be addressed with users and decision-makers when deciding whether to use questionnaires.

A number of additional issues should also be taken into consideration when planning for questionnaire methods, specifically for language program evaluation. For example, will targeted respondents be sufficiently motivated to complete a questionnaire? Will respondents be sufficiently informed to complete the questionnaire (are program experiences recent enough to be recalled accurately)? Do respondents have sufficient language skills to complete the questionnaire (are resources available for translation)? Are respondents culturally disposed to completing questionnaires honestly? Are respondents accessible for questionnaire administration (is contact information available and current)? What are intended users' attitudes toward questionnaire research, generally? Will they be accepting of quantitative data and statistical analysis (Davis 2011)? Per use-focused evaluation guidelines, primary intended users and other key stakeholders need to agree that a questionnaire method is the best choice given the evaluation foci and uses (see chapter 5). Like indicators, methods need to be perceived as appropriate and sufficiently accurate, or findings may be seen as untrustworthy, decreasing the likelihood that information will be used (Davis 2011).

Planning Data Collection with Questionnaires

Like focus groups and interviews, administering a questionnaire involves a series of detailed steps that require careful planning. For evaluation purposes, how the evaluation will be used and by whom are important additional considerations that affect how the questionnaire is designed and implemented.

One of the main pieces of methodological advice for questionnaire research is that researchers should have a clear purpose and explicit set of research questions before beginning questionnaire design. A clearly defined and articulated set of aims helps to create items in a purposeful way so that the information the items gather is both needed and relevant. The same is true for designing questionnaires for evaluation purposes. Evaluators need to have a clear set of indicators to guide the creation of the specific questions and prompts that will gather the relevant information needed to answer evaluation questions and enable evaluation uses. The first step, then, when starting to develop the questionnaire is to have the list of indicators nearby as a reference and to check that every questionnaire item captures information relevant to an evaluation indicator. Evaluators should resist the urge to "fish" for additional information of general interest beyond the scope of the evaluation foci.

Evaluators should also lay out a timeline for when important planning and administration events should happen, as well as a plan for who will have particular questionnaire-development responsibilities. Questionnaires take a nontrivial amount of time to develop, administer, and analyze. Evaluators should be clear about who will draft the questionnaire, how much collaboration will be involved with stakeholders and end-users, who will review the questionnaire prior to administration, how much time they will need to do this, when the best time will be to administer the questionnaire, and when respondents are available. For mailed or online questionnaires, evaluators need to determine how long the administration period will be, including time for extensions (and how many extensions will be needed). For paper-based administrations, data will need to be organized or entered into a spreadsheet by hand, which can be time consuming if there are many respondents. Extra time will be needed for these added tasks (adapted from Davis 2011).

Writing Questionnaire Items

Questionnaire items generally fall into two types: closed-ended (i.e., selected-response) items and open-ended (i.e., constructed-response) items.

Closed-ended or selected-response items provide respondents with a set of predetermined response options that allow them to select answers of their choice. Dichotomous (true/false, yes/no), multiple-choice, and rating-scale formats are the most common closed-ended items. Examples are provided in table 8.1.[1]

Close-ended items have the advantage of being relatively easy to answer, are less likely to be skipped, are relatively easy to summarize or analyze, and allow for statistical analysis. Closed-ended items, however, can be tricky to write in that they can easily bias responses if written poorly.

Open-ended (or constructed-response) items, on the other hand, present no preset answer choices and prompt respondents to answer in their own words. They include short-answer, clarification, or sentence-completion items, which may offer richer data than selected-response items. Examples are provided in table 8.2.[2]

Table 8.1 Types of closed-response questionnaire items

Type	Details	Example
Dichotomous	Two response choices (yes/no, true/false)	Did you study abroad during your studies? • Yes • No
Rating scale	Selecting one of a series of categories organized into a scale	Study abroad improved my language abilities. • Strongly agree • Agree • Neither agree or disagree • Disagree • Strongly disagree • Not applicable
Multiple choice	Multiple response options	Student status: • Freshman • Sophomore • Junior • Senior • Other: _____

Table 8.2 Types of open-response questionnaire items

Type	Details	Example
Short-answer	Free response	What recommendations do you have to improve the program?
Specific	Asks for specific information	What languages have you studied in the past?
Clarification	Attached to closed-response items to clarify the prior response(s)	Please provide comments that will help us understand your ratings.
Sentence completion	Unfinished sentence prompt	One thing I liked about this course is_____.

Open-ended items are advantageous since they can provide a wide range of possible answers, which enables free expression of opinions (Davis 2011). Open-ended items, however, present a number of notable disadvantages for language program evaluation, as noted above. They are time consuming to complete, labor intensive to write, and have an essay-test-like aspect (issues more acute for multilingual respondents). For these reasons, open-response items are prone to be left blank or skipped. Open-response items, then, are usually best for eliciting short, specific responses or for offering opportunities to comment or clarify further on previous closed- or selected-item responses. Certainly, open-response items are useful for asking end-of-questionnaire questions, such as, "What recommendations do you have to improve the program?" or "What are the strengths of the program?" However, they cannot be relied on by themselves to consistently generate thoughtful, extensive comments on such topics. In addition, stakeholders responding to open-response items in a second language may avoid them due to the way in which their answers might reveal their identity.

Writing Useful Items

The usefulness and trustworthiness of information collected via questionnaires relies on well-written items. For example, questionnaire items unrelated to project indicators are unlikely to capture information relevant to the evaluation. In addition, poorly written items can lead to (1) responses or results that are unclear or impossible to interpret, (2) responses that are biased and fail to capture what informants honestly think, or (3) skipped items that provide no information at all. To avoid these pitfalls, the guidelines below provide best practices for writing high-quality questionnaires.[3]

Be Brief

Keep questions as short as possible. Avoid superfluous words or information.

Be Objective

Pay attention to the neutrality of words. Avoid loaded questions, or items that create bias through emotionally charged wording (e.g., "Do you prefer the native-speaking language instructors in the program?" Response: yes/no). Avoid leading questions—that is, item wording that pushes the respondent toward a certain answer (e.g., "The amount of daily homework assigned in our class should be increased" Response: agree/disagree scale). Avoid questions that ask for socially desirable responses, "which either flatter the respondent's self-image or injure his[/her] pride" (e.g., "How many times over the course did you complete your journal on time?"; Warwick and Lininger 1975, 144).

Be Simple

Use words and expressions that are simple, direct, and familiar to targeted respondents. Avoid technical jargon or concepts. Avoid negative or double-negative expressions (e.g., "I don't like grammar-oriented learning" Response: agree/disagree scale). Simplicity is particularly important for multilingual respondents if they are responding in their second language.

Be Specific

Avoid questions for which the respondent does not have an answer (e.g., "Is getting a high grade the main motivation for students?" Better to ask students this question than teachers). Avoid expressing ideas that are too general, too complex, or undefined (e.g., "On average, how many times do you write during the week?" "Write" in this instance is too vague/general). Make the choices for an item exhaustive (e.g., provide an "Other" option).

Sequence Appropriately

Aim for sensible, logical organization and ordering of items (e.g., by theme). To that end, note that "no single question is more crucial than the first one" (Dillman 2000, 92). Make the first question interesting, easy to answer, and applicable to all respondents. Ask interesting questions in the beginning. Place sensitive questions at the end. Number all sections, subsections, and items, and avoid extensive "branching" (e.g., "If yes, go to section 3; if no, …").

Avoid Asking Two Questions in One

Ask about a single point or issue in each item; that is, avoid "double-barreled" questions. Consider the following example: "More funding is needed to improve facilities and salaries" (response: agree/disagree scale). Results for this item are uninterpretable since it would be unknown if they reflected the respondents' views about funding for facilities or salaries. This item should be broken up into two separate items, one asking about facilities and another asking about salaries.

Group Items in Logical Ways

Group items together by content; place related items together. Group items together with the same response format (e.g., place multiple rating responses in a matrix). Provide brief instructions at the beginning of each subsection or group of similar item types.

Rating Scales: Keep Them Short; Offer "Not Applicable" Options; Label All Scale Points

Provide no more than four to five rating options in a scale (e.g., Strongly disagree, Disagree, Neither agree nor disagree, Agree, Strongly agree). Label all response options on a scale (e.g., *avoid* 1 = not useful at all, 2, 3, 4 = very useful). Provide "N/A" (not applicable) or "neutral" options to accurately capture the views of informants who do not have an opinion or for whom the item is irrelevant.

Open-Response: Use Sparingly

Open-ended questions are "easy to ask, [but] difficult to answer" (Oppenheim 1992, 113). Use sparingly.

Open-Response: Use to Probe Respondents' Views of Specific Issues

Open-response items work well if they are not completely open but contain some guidance and ask something specific (Dörnyei and Taguchi 2010).

Additional Considerations of Questionnaire Design

For questionnaires to provide useful information, attention must be paid to questionnaire appearance, length, the introduction, and concluding information.

Appearance

Make the questionnaire visually attractive and user-friendly. Avoid small or difficult-to-read fonts. Use different typeface and highlighting options to emphasize key information (though do so sparingly, without creating garish text). If the questionnaire is paper based, use space economically but avoid cluttered, crowed layouts. In addition, if budget allows, use high-quality printing or copying and copy paper. For online questionnaires, ensure color schemes do not impede clarity of text.

Length

As a general rule, keep the questionnaire as short as possible. Shorter questionnaires are more likely to be completed, which impacts response rates. Design the questionnaire to take no more than five to ten minutes (at the maximum) to complete. For online questionnaires, provide a sense of progress using a questionnaire-completion bar (most online questionnaire platforms offer this option). A progress bar indicates how much of the questionnaire has been completed and how much remains.

Questionnaire Introduction

Be sure to provide an introduction at the beginning of the questionnaire. For online questionnaires, place questions or items on separate, subsequent pages. The introduction should accomplish the following as briefly as possible: explain the questionnaire's purpose, identify the entity or individual(s) administering the questionnaire, explain how the information will be used, provide assurances about confidentiality, state how much time is needed to complete the questionnaire, stress the value of respondents' participation, and provide contact information for respondent queries.

Last Page and Parting Information

At the end of the questionnaire, respondents should be provided with some final, parting information. In online formats, respondents should navigate to a final page separate from the rest of the questionnaire. Concluding or parting information should express gratitude to respondents and provide contact information for any queries about the questionnaire or evaluation project.

Questionnaire Review and Piloting

Once a draft questionnaire is ready, a number of review and piloting strategies are needed to ensure that the instrument is functioning effectively and collecting needed information as intended.

First, have as many stakeholders as possible review and edit the initial draft of the questionnaire. Project users (the highest priority reviewers) and key stakeholders should definitely be asked to review and edit. Before they do, remind them of evaluation questions and uses. To increase instrument quality and reliability, also consult any willing colleagues with questionnaire expertise.

After review and editing, pilot the questionnaire with a few individuals whose profile is similar to those of the intended respondents. Piloting involves trying out questionnaires to identify potential problems with wording, item type, flow, and length. A number of options are available for piloting questionnaires. Evaluators can use a "think-aloud" procedure, which involves asking a pilot respondent to complete the questionnaire verbally and listening for problems based on the respondent's comments. To implement this procedure, (1) target a few participants similar in profile to individuals in the respondent group; (2) explain to the volunteer that they are to verbalize all of their thoughts (i.e., think aloud) as they complete the questionnaire; (3) while the respondent speaks, take notes (or record) to capture details of the participants' feedback, looking in particular for any confusions or misunderstandings of items.

Another pilot option is to conduct a paper-based version of the think-aloud procedure in which pilot respondents are asked to write feedback in the margins of a paper questionnaire. To implement this procedure, (1) provide a paper version of the questionnaire with ample space in the margins and white space between items; (2) ask a variety of individuals (not only targeted respondents) to complete the instrument; (3) ask pilot respondents to complete the questionnaire and write comments on the questionnaire about anything that they find confusing or problematic. Optionally, if the paper questionnaire has been administered to a group, the evaluator can follow with a Q&A session to get group feedback.

The final strategy is to conduct a preadministration with target participants. With large populations, it can be helpful to preadminister the questionnaire to a small, representative group of target respondents. To implement this procedure, (1) administer the questionnaire in exactly the same way as for the live administration; (2) once data are collected, check for potentially problematic response patterns such as items consistently left blank, items consistently answered in unintended ways, or items consistently answered similarly (for which variance is expected). Also review any open-response comments for clues about why items are functioning poorly.

Administering the Questionnaire

When the questionnaire is ready, evaluators will need to decide whether to administer the questionnaire to the entire the population (a census) or to a subgroup of the target population (a sample). Generally, population size and available resources will determine whether to take a census or a sample, though intended uses will affect sampling decisions as well. All things being equal, if the size of the target population is such that every individual can feasibly participate in the questionnaire (with a reasonable expenditure of time and resources), then evaluators may want to send the survey to the entire population. If the population is so large that taking a census is unfeasible, evaluators should consider administering the questionnaire to a selected sample of individuals.

If a given evaluation project calls for the questionnaire to be administered to a subgroup or sample of a particular population (e.g., alumni), the evaluator will need to decide how to select and recruit the needed respondents. One option is to identify all the members of the relevant population (i.e., via a list of names) and randomly select a sample of respondents. Or, if random selection is not possible, the evaluator can select conveniently available individuals (e.g., currently enrolled students, local alumni) or ask participants to recruit more respondents from among their colleagues or classmates. A detailed discussion of sampling approaches (e.g., random/probability, nonprobability/nonrandom techniques) and modes of administration (e.g., mailed, web-based questionnaires) goes beyond the scope of this book. Readers are encouraged to consult the references listed at the end of this chapter for more information.[4]

Questionnaire Administration: Response Rate

An important consideration in questionnaire administration is to do everything possible to ensure a high response rate, particularly if the evaluation project requires that results accurately reflect the views of stakeholder populations. Again, "response rate" refers to the proportion of respondents who completed and submitted their questionnaires (i.e., the number of completed questionnaires divided by the total number administered). As a general rule, evaluators should aim for as high a questionnaire response rate as possible, especially if decision-makers want to make claims about questionnaire findings for an entire population (e.g., undergraduates enrolled in required foreign language courses). Whether the evaluator has taken a sample or a census, questionnaires results are regarded as untrustworthy if they do not capture a majority of respondent views. When response rates are excessively low, rather than capturing a representative distribution of views in the population, questionnaire results may be biased by the opinions of the self-selecting respondent group (e.g., strongly opinionated individuals who are, for some reason, eager to respond).

A number of strategies can be implemented to increase response rates. The first and best strategy is to conduct an in-person, group administration. Wherever possible, take advantage of situations where respondents are a captive audience—that is, physically present and grouped together during a weekly class or regular meeting. In such situations, administer a paper-based questionnaire during regularly scheduled meeting times.

More commonly, questionnaires will be administered online (e.g., via email), and a number of strategies can help to increase the likelihood of response.[5]

Create a Respondent-Friendly Questionnaire
Write clear questions, use appropriate question order, observe visual layout recommendations, and most importantly, keep the questionnaire short (ten minutes or less).

Personalize Correspondence
Address respondents individually on the questionnaire form or invitation correspondence by name if possible (try using a "mail merge" to make this process easier). Send a personalized invitation from a high-ranking manager or administrator.

Provide Assurances of Confidentiality
Assure respondents that their answers will be kept confidential. Relatedly, be transparent about who will use the informants' responses and how the information will be used.

Determine an Optimal (E)Mail-Out Date and Administration Period
Administer questionnaires when respondents will be more likely to respond (avoid busy periods, holidays, etc.). Allow enough time to complete the questionnaire (e.g., ten days to two weeks for the initial administration period). Allow sufficient scheduling time for multiple follow-up reminders (two reminders maximum). Be clear about deadlines for when collection will stop.

Be Clear about How Long the Questionnaire Takes to Complete
Again, keep the questionnaire short; ideally, it should take less than ten minutes to complete. Let respondents know up front how long the questionnaire will take. If the questionnaire is very short (e.g., five minutes), advertise this fact prominently.

Explain the Importance of the Questionnaire
Make it clear that respondents' views are crucially important for the evaluation project and that their responses are valued. Include this information in the invitation email.

Provide Questionnaire Instructions
Explain briefly how to navigate through the questionnaire and how to submit it. Include instructions for each section of the questionnaire if applicable.

Send Multiple Notifications
Send a prenotification email or letter (requesting participation in advance) that is brief, personalized, positively worded, aimed at building anticipation, and arriving a few days before administration. In addition, send follow-up reminders. Without follow-up reminders, response rates are twenty to forty percent lower (Dillman 2000). Track nonresponders and contact them specifically in follow-up notifications (though note ethical considerations regarding confidentiality).

Strategies for Posted or Mailed Questionnaires
Use a cover letter (less than a page, explaining why the survey is important). Supply a stamped, self-addressed envelope. Put the mailing address somewhere on the questionnaire (see "parting information" above).

Evaluation Scenario: Example Questionnaire

In the eleventh-grade Chinese telecollaboration evaluation (scenario 3), evaluation question 1 asks, "How satisfied are students and teachers with the telecollaboration program?" The indicators for the question include (1) students' and teachers' levels of satisfaction with the program, (2) perceived usefulness of the program for learning, (3) level of engagement and motivation during telecollaboration sessions, (4) intent to pursue future Chinese study, and (5) enrollment in twelfth-grade Chinese courses. Students are a clear informant group that evaluators would want to survey in order to capture their views on the effectiveness of the program (for learning), overall satisfaction with the program, and felt levels of motivation and engagement during the course. Since there are twenty students in the course, a questionnaire is a good way to capture opinions from this relatively large group of informants. Also, since the relevant indicators are relatively specific (satisfaction, usefulness for learning, engagement, motivation), they lend themselves well to questionnaire-type items.

In addition, we might imagine that during a focus group with a smaller group of students, student opinions about the course depended on individual factors, such as whether the student had a Chinese cultural heritage, whether Chinese was spoken in the home, future plans for Chinese travel, or interest in Chinese culture. Also, some students with prior computer-assisted language-learning experience seemed better able to use the technology effectively and get the most out of the telecollaboration interactions and activities. The evaluators in this fictional situation, then, have decided to analyze the questionnaire results in terms of these individual differences between students.

The evaluation is also interested in the effectiveness of the course for student learning (evaluation question 2). The evaluators and users have identified achievement of student learning outcomes as a key indicator of course effectiveness. In addition to other tests and assessments, the evaluators also decided to collect student self-assessment information, asking respondents to rate their abilities to perform the course "can-do" learning outcomes.

In such a scenario, the following sample questionnaire (figure 8.1) could be used to elicit information from student informants on abilities, satisfaction, motivation, engagement, and usefulness for language learning. To maintain a high response rate and ensure results are representative of the full group of students, the survey would probably best be administered on the last day of the telecollaboration course in the computer lab where the telecollaboration interactions happened.

Notes

1. Adapted from Davis (2011).
2. Ibid.
3. Adapted from Iarossi (2006).
4. For additional information on developing questionnaires for evaluation see Brown (2001); Dillman, Smyth, and Christian (2014); Davis (2011); Dörnyei and Taguchi (2010); and Patten (2001).
5. Adapted from Davis (2011).

INTRODUCTION

You are receiving this survey because you recently participated in the eleventh-grade Chinese telecollaboration course.

This questionnaire is being conducted by the school language instructors. The questionnaire asks about the usefulness of the program for your language learning. Your responses will be used to improve the program.

The questionnaire will take approximately five to ten minutes to complete.

Your participation is voluntary. Your responses will be kept confidential and will not include details that could be associated with your identity.

If you have any questions regarding the survey, please contact [CONTACT PERSON NAME] at [CONTACT EMAIL/PHONE].

Section I. BACKGROUND INFORMATION

1. Does anybody in your home speak Chinese as a native or first language?
   ☐ Yes   ☐ No

2. Which of the following best describes your reason for learning Chinese? Choose all that apply.
   ☐ Communicating with family and relatives
   ☐ Interest in Chinese culture
   ☐ Future plans to travel to or study in China
   ☐ College credit
   ☐ Other: _____

3. Did you have any experiences with computer-assisted language learning with a speaking partner prior to this course (e.g., online tutoring, online exchange)?
   ☐ Yes   ☐ No (If "No," go to section II)

4. If you answered "Yes" above, what communication tools have you used?
   ☐ Social network (e.g., Facebook, Twitter)
   ☐ Email
   ☐ Chat
   ☐ Discussion forum
   ☐ Video conferencing (e.g., Skype, Google Hangouts, FaceTime)
   ☐ Other: _____

(continued)

Section II. PROGRAM EFFECTIVENESS

1. Please rate how useful the different parts of the course were for your Chinese language learning:

USEFULNESS FOR LANGUAGE LEARNING	Not useful at all	Minimally useful	Somewhat useful	Very useful
1. Interaction with Chinese language partner				
2. Reading the shared text				
3. Group class discussion after partner interaction				
4. Learning diary				
5. Feedback from language instructor				

Please provide comments to help us understand your ratings:

2. Overall, how useful was the telecollaboration course for learning Chinese?
    - ☐ Very useful
    - ☐ Somewhat useful
    - ☐ Minimally useful
    - ☐ Not useful at all

Please provide comments to help us understand your ratings:

3. Please indicate the extent to which you agree or disagree with the following statements:

TECHNOLOGY	Strongly disagree	Disagree	Neither agree or disagree	Agree	Strongly agree
1. The telecollaboration technology was easy to use.					
2. There was good video quality during the interactions.					
3. There was good sound quality during the interactions.					
4. The technology worked reliably.					

COURSE EXPERIENCE	Strongly disagree	Disagree	Neither agree or disagree	Agree	Strongly agree
1. The course was interesting.					
2. The course made language learning fun.					
3. I enjoyed the interactions with my speaking partner.					
4. I found discussions with my partner interesting.					
5. I would take a similar course again if available.					
6. I would recommend this course to a friend.					

Please provide comments to help us understand your ratings:

4. Please rate the extent to which you can do the following in Chinese:

CHINESE COMPETENCIES	Not at all	Poorly	Okay	Well	Very well
1. Talk about family and personal history					
2. Talk about likes, dislikes, and opinions					
3. Talk about hobbies, personal interests					
4. Talk about future plans for study or vacation					
5. Talk about issues important for young people in the United States and/or China					
6. Talk about events and characters in the shared text					
7. Ask for clarification when I don't understand					
8. Restate what I want to say if my partner doesn't understand					
9. Make myself understood, even if I make mistakes					
10. Interact appropriately, politely					

(continued)

Please provide comments to help us understand your ratings:

```
┌──────────────────────────────────────────────┐
│                                              │
│                                              │
│                                              │
└──────────────────────────────────────────────┘
```

5. What is your overall level satisfaction with the Chinese telecollaboration course?
   ☐ Very satisfied
   ☐ Somewhat satisfied
   ☐ Neutral
   ☐ Somewhat unsatisfied
   ☐ Very unsatisfied

6. What suggestions do you have to improve the course?

```
┌──────────────────────────────────────────────┐
│                                              │
│                                              │
│                                              │
└──────────────────────────────────────────────┘
```

THANK YOU

Thank you for completing this questionnaire. If you have any questions about the evaluation, please contact [CONTACT PERSON NAME] at [CONTACT EMAIL/PHONE].

9

Analyzing Evaluation Data

JOHN McE. DAVIS

IN THIS CHAPTER, WE provide introductory advice for analyzing and interpreting evaluation information. We do so by specifically focusing on two data-collection strategies used in the eleventh-grade Chinese telecollaboration scenario: the student focus group and the student questionnaire. For each tool, we describe strategies for summarizing the data and interpreting the results (using Microsoft Excel). We also emphasize the key point that evaluation data analysis and interpretation *must be guided by project evaluation questions.* Evaluators must take special care to ensure that the conclusions they draw from the evaluation results provide answers directly related to project questions and uses. In addition, we provide guidance for ensuring that analysis and interpretation are systematic processes that lead to trustworthy evidence. Finally, we offer some techniques to help ensure that data analysis and interpretation support evaluation usefulness.

Analysis versus Interpretation

We use the term "analysis" in this chapter to refer to the process of organizing and summarizing evaluation information so that conclusions can be drawn about what the data mean and how they answer evaluation questions. For example, numerical analysis of questionnaire data would involve calculations to determine frequencies and percentages of particular responses so that the evaluator and users can see easily what the data suggest about respondents' views. For comments data, analysis typically involves identifying and tracking recurrent themes arising in respondents' comments from focus groups or interviews, counting how many times a theme arises, and then listing the tallies and proportions for each theme to get a sense of frequent and important ideas. When data are analyzed and ready for interpretation, they become the "results" of the data-collection process.

Interpretation is slightly different. Interpretation is the process of drawing conclusions from the analyzed data to give the results meaning. Interpretation can be thought of as a way to answer the "So what?" test. When questionnaire, focus-group, interview, or assessment results are in hand, how do they matter to the evaluation? What do the results mean? What story do the results seem to tell? What answers do the data suggest in response to the evaluation questions? Interpretation is the final step in the evaluation that synthesizes the results into the key evaluation findings.

In the remainder of the chapter we discuss two of the three data-collection methods from the Chinese telecollaboration scenario: a fictional questionnaire sent to students and a fictional student focus-group session. We explore both of these methods—presenting example data along the way—to show how numerical and textual data can be systematically analyzed and interpreted to answer evaluation questions.

Trustworthiness of Analysis and Interpretation

Before looking at strategies for how to analyze and interpret data, it is important to note that both processes need to be conducted at a high level of quality and rigor to ensure data trustworthiness. Data trustworthiness is crucially important for evaluation to be useful (see chapter 5). Stakeholders and users need to feel that the findings from the evaluation are accurate and free from bias and other problems of measurement. Important decisions cannot be made on the basis of faulty or untrustworthy information. Summaries and interpretations of evaluation data, then, must be conducted carefully and systematically using particular strategies to avoid bias and other errors.

Recall from the previous chapters the different ways in which bias and other types of inaccuracy can creep into data design and collection processes. For example, questionnaire items might be written poorly such that they influence respondents to answer in ways that they might not otherwise had the item been written differently. Or, perhaps an interviewer shows excessive disapproval or enthusiasm during an interview, which changes how the interviewee responds, resulting in the evaluation no longer collecting accurate information on interviewee opinions.

In this chapter, we highlight threats to data accuracy and trustworthiness that can happen during the analysis and interpretation phases of the evaluation. When analyzing numerical or comments data, special care must be taken to summarize the data in a way that avoids omitting information, distorting information, or otherwise failing to capture important trends or features in the data. For example, having only one evaluator identify themes in comments data may not be enough to ensure that important, recurring ideas have been captured accurately. Or, for numerical data, reporting only an average for rating items (and failing to provide standard deviations) may not give a complete picture of how students or teachers view a particular program issue of interest.

The same is true with interpretation. Unsystematic, incomplete, or erroneous interpretation can lead to conclusions that fail to follow from results in logical ways. A simple example is simply missing or forgetting important details in results, which leads to faulty conclusions based on an incomplete review of evaluation data. Or, when interpreting comments, undue weight might be given to minority views from a single source over high-frequency views appearing consistently from a variety of sources. Or, an undisciplined set of interpretations may have lost sight of the project evaluation questions and led to conclusions unrelated to the evaluation purpose. Throughout the remainder of the chapter we describe strategies and checks that can be used to help ensure data are analyzed accurately, and that users view interpretations as appropriate and warranted.

Analyzing Numerical Information

As noted previously, the first and most important priority in analyzing evaluation data is to keep the evaluation questions firmly in mind. In the case of the Chinese telecollaboration scenario, two evaluation questions were posed:

1. How satisfied are students and teachers with the telecollaboration program?
2. How effective is the Chinese telecollaboration program for student learning?

Student Questionnaire: Analyzing Selected-Response Items

One important set of analyses needed in this scenario will focus on the selected-response questionnaire items. In order to summarize the data, simple mathematical calculations will be needed to provide an easy-to-read visualization of students' responses and to get a clear sense of satisfaction and program effectiveness.

Prior to this step, however, an important analysis that should always be conducted for questionnaire results is the response rate. The response rate is the proportion of people who responded to the questionnaire. The response rate is calculated by dividing the number of people who completed the questionnaire by the number of people sent the questionnaire. As noted in chapter 8, response rates are an important piece of evidence that show how representative the questionnaire results are of the population of respondents. In order to calculate the response rate, evaluators should always know how many people were sent an evaluation questionnaire. Mailing questionnaires to unknown numbers of recipients makes it impossible to know what proportion of the population is captured in the responding group. Evaluators must consider this issue carefully and be aware of how users will react to an unknown (or low) response rate. High response rates (around seventy-five percent or more) provide strong evidence that the questionnaire results represent the views of the student or teacher population in the program. Even if the response rate is low (e.g., fifty percent or less), it can still be reported, and users can make up their minds about whether to act on the questionnaire findings. Without any response-rate results whatsoever, users interested in the generalizability of results will have no way to judge whether findings can be trusted.

In the eleventh-grade Chinese telecollaboration scenario, recall that the questionnaire was administered in class. Let us imagine, then, that there are ten students enrolled in the Chinese telecollaboration course, but only eight attended on the day of the survey. Eight respondents out of ten possible respondents equals a response rate of eighty percent for this student questionnaire. Again, response rates for evaluation questionnaires should always be reported. In this case, the response rate is quite high and evaluators could feel confident that the results of the questionnaire capture the majority of student views on the telecollaboration course.

Preparing Numerical Questionnaire Data for Analysis

Since the questionnaire was administered online in class via the class desktop computers (using a web-based application, such as SurveyMonkey, Qualtrics, or Google Forms), a spreadsheet would be downloaded capturing all of the students' responses (see the example Excel spreadsheet in figure 9.1). Note that the columns in the spreadsheet list the responses to a particular item, and the rows reflect the responses of a single participant. The top rows list the item prompts and multiple-choice options. In addition, good data analysis practice involves inserting an extra column in the first column, labelling it "ID," and giving each respondent a unique identification number.

Before conducting any analyses, evaluators should check the data entries to make sure there are no peculiarities. For example, someone may have entered an age of two hundred years old, or a respondent might have completed the first few items and then exited the questionnaire, leaving the rest of the row without any data. These errors can impact calculations in ways that distort results, and the data set should be inspected to make sure there are no strange or missing patterns of response.

Another concern related to comments data is that they may reveal either the respondent's or another program stakeholder's identity. Sometimes respondents will name an instructor or classmate. Also, a respondent's multilingual identity can be revealed in their writing style. Thus, data should be checked for personally identifying information and edited to protect confidentiality (either replacing individuals' names with "[NAME]" or removing certain comments altogether).

Analyzing Numerical Questionnaire Data

Once these checks are concluded, the next step is to start the analyses for each questionnaire item. Looking at the Chinese telecollaboration questionnaire from chapter 8, there are four types of item to review: dichotomous items (yes/no), multiple-choice items, rating-scale items, and open-ended comments items. In the following sections, we provide brief examples of how to analyze selected-response items using fictional example data and introductory Excel techniques (analyzing open-ended items is discussed later in the chapter).

Dichotomous Items

"Does anybody in your home speak Chinese as a native/first language?"

The response data for the first item in the Chinese telecollaboration questionnaire should be arranged as depicted in figure 9.1. The primary goal in analyzing this type of item will be to show both the *number* of respondents in the course with or without a Chinese cultural heritage as well as the *proportion or percentage* of these respondents out of the entire responding group. The main interest of the analysis will be in how much there is of one type of response versus another. Both counts and percentages are needed for this purpose. To this end, a few simple Excel commands and steps can be used.

1. Count the total number of respondents for this item. In cell B11, type =COUNTA(B3:B10). This formula will show the number of nonblank cells from B3 to B10 in cell B11, indicating the number of respondents that selected a response for this item (i.e., 8).

2. Count the number of "Yes" and "No" responses. In cell B12, type =COUNTIF(B3:B10,"Yes"). In cell B13, type =COUNTIF(B3:B10,"No"). These formulas will count the number of "Yes" and "No" responses and return those values in cells B12 and B13 ("Yes" = 1; "No" = 7).

	A	B	C	D	E	F	G	H	I
1	ID	1. Does anybody in your home speak Chinese	2. Which of the following best describes your reason for learning Chinese?					3. Did you have any experiences with computer-assisted	4. If you what cor you used
2			Communicating with family and relatives	Interest in Chinese culture	Future plans to travel/study in China	College credit	Other:		Social ne
3	1	Yes	Communicat	Interest in Chinese culture				Yes	
4	2	No		Interest in Chinese culture				No	
5	3	No			Future plans to travel/study i			No	
6	4	No				College credit		No	
7	5	No		Interest in Chinese culture				No	
8	6	No		Interest in Chinese cultur		College credit		No	
9	7	No		Interest in Chinese culture				No	
10	8	No				College credit		No	
11									
12									

Sheet1 | Sheet 2 | Sheet 3 | (+)

Ready

Figure 9.1 Eleventh-grade Chinese telecollaboration scenario

3. Calculate the percentage of "Yes" and "No" responses. In cell B14, type =B12/8. In cell B15, type =B12/8. These formulas will return the quotients in cells B14 and B15. Click on "%" in the Excel ribbon to transform these values into percentages ("Yes" = 12.5%; "No" = 87.5%).[1]

4. Create a table showing results. Somewhere in the Excel worksheet or another document, create a table that captures both the percentages and the response counts (and totals of each) as shown in table 9.1.

These results can also be visualized using a pie or bar chart if desired since both provide a helpful visual comparison of differences in proportions of response. At the very least, however, a table capturing the results as shown in table 9.1 should be created somewhere in the analysis documentation (and possibly included in a report appendix).[2]

Table 9.1 Example analysis of a dichotomous questionnaire item

1. Does anybody in your home speak Chinese as a native or first language?

Response	n	%
No	7	87.5
Yes	1	12.5
Total	8	100.0

Multiple-Choice Items

"Which of the following best describes your reason for learning Chinese?"

Analyzing this type of selected-response item (and others like it in the Chinese tele-collaboration example) should also show the frequencies *and* proportions of each of the selected options. To do so, the steps noted above for dichotomous items can be repeated, with some additions.

1. Count the number of responses in columns C through G. In cells C11, D11, E11, F11, and G11, use the =COUNTIF(range, value) formula to count the number of respondents who selected a particular option.
2. Sum the total number of selections. In any free cell, type =SUM(C11:G11). This formula will add up all the values in C11 to G11 (i.e., 10).
3. Calculate percentages for each of the option selections. In a free cell in each option column, divide each of the counts computed in step 2 by 10. For example, for column C ("Communicating with family and relatives"), in a free cell, type =C11/10. Click the percentage option in the Excel tool ribbon (=10%). Repeat for the remaining selection options.
4. Create a table showing results. Again, it is important to show both counts and percentages (and totals) for each of the multiple-choice response options. Also, rank item results from the most frequent or highest percentage to the lowest so that trends can be spotted quickly (see table 9.2).

Again, different data-visualization strategies can be used to show the results in more appealing or interpretable ways, but the data should be reported as shown in table 9.2 somewhere in the analysis documentation.

Rating-Scale Items

"Please rate how useful the different parts of the course were for your Chinese language learning."

A common item type used in evaluation questionnaires is a rating-scale item where respondents have to select a response from a number of options along a scale. For example, in the Chinese telecollaboration scenario, students are asked to rate the usefulness of various course elements ("Interaction with Chinese language partner," "Reading the shared

Table 9.2 Example analysis of a multiple-choice questionnaire item

2. Which of the following best describes your reason for learning Chinese?

Response	n	%
Interest in Chinese culture	5	50
College credit	3	30
Future plans to travel to or study in China	1	10
Communicating with family and relatives	1	10
Other	0	0
Total	10	100.0

text," "Group class discussion after partner interaction," "Learning diary," and "Feedback from language instructor"). Students are asked to rate these items as "Not useful at all," "Minimally useful," "Somewhat useful," or "Very useful." A downloaded spreadsheet for this type of data would be arranged as depicted in figure 9.2.

A number of analysis options are available to evaluators for this type of item. However, we recommend a simple approach using the techniques and Excel commands already discussed. Since users are interested in ascertaining the usefulness of the program for student learning, they will want to quickly understand student opinions on the more or less useful course elements.

As with the analyses above, evaluators should calculate the frequency and proportion of each rating for each item. In addition to counts and frequencies, item descriptive statistics can be calculated to shed light on program usefulness. Average item ratings (or mean ratings) and standard deviations can be used for this purpose. In order to calculate these statistics, however, the textual responses in each cell in figure 9.2 will need to be transformed into numerical values that capture where a rating falls on the rating scale. For example, all "Not useful at all" ratings should be given a value of 1; "Minimally useful" ratings should be changed to 2; and so on.[3]

AB4	▾	× ✓ _fx_			
	O	P	Q	R	S	T
1	1. Please rate how useful the different parts of the course were for your Chinese language learning:				Please provide comments to help us understand your
2	1. Interaction with Chinese language partner	2. Reading the shared text	3. Group class discussion after partner	4. Learning diary	5. Feedback from language instructor	
3	Minimally usefu	Somewha	Very useful	Not usefu	Somewhat	I really liked t
4	Very useful	Minimall	Minimally	Minimall	Minimally useful	
5	Very useful	Somewha	Not useful	Not usefu	Somewhat	I neve used tl
6	Somewhat usef	Minimall	Minimally	Minimall	Minimally useful	
7	Very useful	Minimall	Not useful	Minimall	Minimally	Please provid
8	Somewhat usef	Somewha	Minimally	Minimall	Somewhat useful	
9	Very useful	Very usef	Minimally	Not usefu	Very useful	
10	Somewhat usef	Somewha	Not useful	Minimall	Somewhat useful	
11						

| Sheet1 | Sheet 2 | Sheet 3 | ⊕ |

● Figure 9.2 Excerpt of downloaded spreadsheet questionnaire responses

While descriptive statistics can be useful for analyzing evaluation rating-scale items, we propose that reporting counts and percentages for item ratings is a more accurate and meaningful approach to analyzing this type of data for evaluation purposes. If evaluators wish to show means and standard deviations (and other statistics such as the median, mode, etc.), this is fine, but we recommend that they be shown along with percentages and counts as well.

The analysis of rating items should focus on showing clear patterns of response on students' ratings of usefulness:

1. Count the total numbers of responses for all possible ratings for a given rating-scale item. In a free cell in column O, type =COUNTIF(O3:O10,"Not useful at all"); in another free cell in column O, type =COUNTIF(O3:O10,"Minimally useful") and so on (for all response options). Repeat for each column/item.
2. Calculate percentages for each of the option selections. Divide each of the rating frequencies by the number of responses for each item (8).
3. Create a table showing results. In table 9.3, counts and frequencies of all rating selections are shown. Note that the highest percentages have been bolded. Also, in this instance, items have been listed from the highest to lowest mean item usefulness rating. Thus, the table shows items ranked by perceived usefulness, a helpful way to quickly understand trends.

Given the amount of information in table 9.3, data visualization might be needed to help users and stakeholders quickly understand results. For rating scales that produce complex tables like the one above, data visualization can simplify interpretation, as shown in figure 9.3. Note that the useful ratings ("Very useful" and "Somewhat useful) are colored the same, as are the non-useful items ("Minimally useful" and "Not useful at all") to show quickly interpretable contrasts between useful and unuseful ratings.

At this stage of the analysis, the results are suggestive of (1) the types of students taking the course, (2) why they are taking the course, and (3) the aspects of the course students find most and least useful. All of these sources of data are relevant to the evaluation project since they provide evidence to answer evaluation question 2 on the usefulness of the program for student learning. In addition, given the interest in usefulness for students, there might be a number of additional possibilities for data analysis in this scenario. For example, a potentially relevant issue would be whether different types of participants are benefiting from the program in different ways. Do learners with a Chinese cultural heritage, for example, perform differently, and are they more engaged? If this concern became relevant to the evaluation (according to users), the same analyses noted above could be conducted again, though this time separating the data into different groups: those with a Chinese cultural heritage versus those without. Interpretation of the results would look for whether there were any notably different patterns of response between the two groups. The important point to remember, however, is that analyses should always have some demonstrable relevance to an evaluation question.

The next steps in the Chinese telecollaboration evaluation would be to complete the analyses of the other questionnaire items and synthesize all of the results into a number of project-relevant conclusions (i.e., interpretation). This process would include, of course,

Table 9.3 Example bar chart for rating-scale questionnaire item

1. Please rate how useful the different parts of the course were for your Chinese language learning.

Response	Not useful at all		Minimally useful		Somewhat useful		Very useful	
	n	%	n	%	n	%	n	%
1. Interaction with Chinese language partner	0	0	1	10	3	30	4	40
2. Reading the shared text	0	0	3	30	4	40	1	10
5. Feedback from language instructor	0	0	3	30	4	40	1	10
3. Group class discussion after partner interaction	3	30	4	40	0	0	1	10
4. Learning diary	3	30	5	50	0	0	0	0

Usefulness of course features for Chinese language learning:

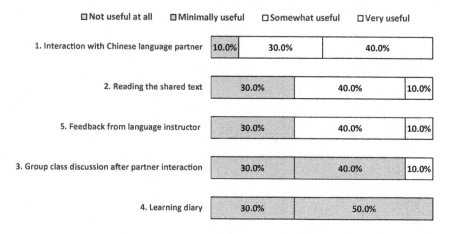

☐ Not useful at all   ☐ Minimally useful   ☐ Somewhat useful   ☐ Very useful

1. Interaction with Chinese language partner	10.0%	30.0%	40.0%
2. Reading the shared text	30.0%	40.0%	10.0%
5. Feedback from language instructor	30.0%	40.0%	10.0%
3. Group class discussion after partner interaction	30.0%	40.0%	10.0%
4. Learning diary	30.0%	50.0%	

Figure 9.3 Example bar chart for rating-scale questionnaire item

analyzing informant comments from the open-ended questionnaire items, focus-group responses, and interviewee comments, a topic we address next.

Analyzing Comments and Textual Information: Focus Groups

The next important data-analysis task for the Chinese telecollaboration evaluation would be to analyze the various comments-type data from the student focus groups, instructor interviews, and student questionnaire comments.

Before this process begins, however, the data should be prepared for analysis. There are a number of qualitative analysis methods and tools available to help prepare textual data for review.[4] Here we suggest a few simple data-preparation and analysis strategies for fictional focus-group data using Excel spreadsheets.

Our approach to analysis of textual data is based on two assumptions:

1. The primary interest of evaluation users will be in knowing about common, prevailing themes and frequently occurring views from various evaluation informants.
2. Analysis of comments will need to be rendered in such a way that users can easily identify and track common themes across numerous comments from numerous individuals.

We note that there are alternative approaches to analyzing qualitative data such that the above assumptions may not apply. For example, users may be interested in any and all improvement-oriented feedback, and any helpful suggestion—even if a minority view—will be of interest. However, in our experience, evaluation users typically want to know if an idea or observation is shared by a majority of informants since common views tend to suggest something notable happening in the program.[5]

Preparing Questionnaire Comments Data for Analysis

As with numerical analysis, the first step in analyzing comments is to display the data in an organized way that allows the evaluator to draw conclusions easily (e.g., in a matrix). One possibility is to organize the data in the way captured in figure 9.4.

Figure 9.4 shows the student focus-group comments listed within an Excel spreadsheet. Note that a single comment is listed in a single cell. Notice further that the focus-group prompt is listed in column A (in cell A35, "Tell us what you like most about talking with your language partners in China"). Other focus-group prompts would be listed further above and below in the sheet in the same column. Interview and open-ended questionnaire items can be arranged similarly. In column B, a unique ID has been assigned to each comment. In column C, each student comment responding to the prompt in A35 is listed in a single cell. This method of data display helps arrange the comments so that they can be coded easily. Coding is a process of developing and assigning labels to each comment in order to categorize important, recurrent themes in the data.

Before starting the coding approach depicted in figure 9.4 (the codes are listed in the first row in columns O–Q), the evaluator should first read through all the comments to

	A	B	C	O	P	Q
1	QUESTION	#	COMMENT	Effective - Interaction	Effective - Authentic speech	Effective - Authentic listening practice
35	Tell us what you like most about talking with your language partners in China.	34	RS: Well what I like best is that it's real communication with a real speaker of the language and It's pretty clear when what I've said isn't understood. So I have to try again and maybe say it a different way. Or maybe I have to figure out if it's my pronunciation or something. It's good. The pressure's on to be understood.	1		
36		35	PS: Yeah I agree. But also I like learning how people really talk and people our age as well. It's hard to learn that from books and in a classroom. I learned some slang from my partner. That was helpful I liked that.	1	1	
37		36	HJ: Yeah I liked that aspect too. Even though I hear a lot of Chinese at home I liked hearing the different accents and how people my age from Shanghai talk.		1	1
38		37	BG: Right chatting really helped with listening. I really had to concentrate to understand what was being said by my partner			1
39		38	RS: That's right I agree with that.			1
40		39	PS: Yeah the biggest improvement I made was my listening ability			1
41			Total	2	2	4

● Figure 9.4 Example Excel spreadsheet for analyzing focus group data

make sure there are no statements identifying individuals (e.g., respondents referring to instructors or other students by name). The data should be cleaned by omitting identifying information and replacing with either ellipses or with "[NAME]" in the place of an individual's name.

Analyzing Comments Questionnaire Data

Once the data are clean and the spreadsheet has been arranged as in figure 9.4, the coding process can begin. "Codes" are short phrases or acronyms that summarize and signify a specific idea from the data. For example, consider comment 34 from figure 9.4:

"RS: Well what I like best is that it's real communication with a real speaker of the language and It's pretty clear when what I've said isn't understood. So I have to try again and maybe say it a different way. Or maybe I have to figure out if it's my pronunciation or something. It's good. The pressure's on to be understood."

Notice that the code "Effective – Interaction" has been assigned to this comment in cell O35 since it captures the essence of this particular participant's statement relevant to the evaluation question (i.e., how interaction is a specific aspect of the course that is helpful for student learning). Coding, then, is an essential process in evaluation textual analysis in that it involves categorizing comments into a set of labels or themes that can then be counted or sorted to better understand notable patterns of response.

In figure 9.4, notice that an evaluator has read through the data set and created a set of codes, which they have entered in the first row. In addition, where a particular code appears to match what was said in a comment, a "1" is entered in the relevant cell under the corresponding code column and in line with the corresponding comment row. Moreover, a 1 has been entered more than once for a single comment in a different column. For example, comment 36 has been coded as "Effective – Authentic speech" and "Effective – Authentic listening practice" since both codes are relevant to this respondent's remark.

This process of assigning 1s to cells where a code matches a comment is a way of keeping track of recurrent themes and tallying the number of times a particular theme arises. To that end, note in row 41 the set of values at the bottom of each code column. These values reflect the total number of times a code was assigned to a comment. In each of the cells in row 41 at the bottom of each column, the coder has typed the following formula: =SUM(CELL:CELL). For example, at the bottom of column O (code = "Effective – Learning from classmates"), the evaluator would have typed =SUM(O2:O40). This simple formula adds up all the 1s in column O, thereby providing a sense of how frequently-noted that particular idea was compared to the other codes. In this way, evaluators can see the prevalence of particular views relevant to the evaluation questions.

Creating and Assigning Codes to Evaluation Comments Data

How can the codes depicted in figure 9.4 be created (and created in a trustworthy way)? We suggest two methods to help ensure that (1) the process of *creating* the codes produces categories that are *accurate* and that correspond well to concepts in the raw data, and (2) the process of *assigning* codes is *consistent* and faithful to ideas in respondents' comments.

Coding Method 1: Two Coders

1. Step 1: Creating the coding scheme. One of the evaluators randomly selects a sample of the comments from the entire interview data set.
2. Two evaluators/coders independently develop codes for the subset of randomly selected comments. Coding involves reading through comments, creating codes as needed (for example, the set of codes in the first row in columns O–Q), and adding additional codes periodically to the next free cell in the first row. In figure 9.4, the coder would have put their first code in D1; for the next code they conceived (either for the same comment, or for a subsequent comment), they would enter it in E1, and so on.
3. Focus on evaluation questions. When assigning codes, the coders/evaluators should have the research questions clearly in mind and should create labels that capture concepts directly relevant to the evaluation. Note in figure 9.4 how the codes in row 1 all have something to do with the effectiveness of the course for student learning, which relates directly to evaluation question 2.
4. When the sampled comments are coded, the coders/evaluators meet and compare their codes. Evaluators then merge their coding schemes, negotiating and resolving any differences. In this way, the coders collaboratively create a checked final coding scheme to be applied to the rest of the data.
5. Step 2: Code the remaining comments. Both evaluators use the coding scheme from step 1 to code all the remaining comments.
6. When complete, coders compare their completed analyses and resolve discrepancies through discussion and negotiation.

Coding Method 2: One Coder

1. Step 1: If only one coder is available, the sole coder/evaluator randomly selects a sample of the comments.
2. As in method 1, the evaluator codes the sample of the comments.
3. The evaluator/coder waits for a week or so. After a week, the evaluator returns to the same subset of comments and codes these comments again, without looking at the codes they created the week before.
4. When the second coding is done, the evaluator compares the two coding schemes created a week apart and synthesizes the two into single coding scheme.
5. Step 2: The coder/evaluator codes the remainder of the comments. If there is time, the coder/evaluator waits a week and codes the remainder of comments again and checks to see if the codings at time 1 and time 2 are similar. The coder then synthesizes and resolves any differences using their best judgment about which codings capture important trends in the data best.

One thing to note in figure 9.4 is how each comment starts with a short acronym. For example, in cell C36, "PS: Yeah I agree…." The acronyms serve a particular purpose. It can be helpful to know if the same respondent is repeatedly mentioning the same point during a focus group or in a questionnaire. If so, the analysis should avoid coding the same idea again and again as if it were being made by different individuals. Assigning the same code repeatedly would give the false impression of a common idea or frequent theme when in fact it is the view of a single individual. A strategy to avoid this is for a notetaker to transcribe participants' remarks and provide a notation for each participant (that does not reveal their identity) using simple acronyms that denote, say, the clothing of a given speaker (PS = plaid shirt, HJ = herringbone jacket, etc.).

Once the first analysis is completed, coding a second or third time is recommended to refine, combine, and reduce the number of codes. Reviewing and revising the analysis helps to omit redundancies, clarify overlapping categories, and otherwise sharpen the conceptual distinctions between codes. Analysis at this stage is an iterative, repeated, cyclical process of coding and recoding, trying to capture all the relevant categories and subcategories present in the data. The process should be repeated until nothing else surfaces (i.e., aiming for saturation). Further, the analysis process will commonly produce a handful of low-frequency codes (one or two codings only), which add little if any meaningful information to the evaluation. Low-frequency codes can either be combined into superordinate categories or omitted altogether.

Once coding is complete, evaluators should consider creating a summary table that lists the codes and their frequencies and other relevant information. In addition, it can be useful to include a few notable quotes in the table as prototypical examples of an important theme. Table 9.4 provides a simple example summary table showing qualitative results that might be derived from a spreadsheet similar to figure 9.4. Note that the themes are ranked from most to least frequent. Additional options for organizing the results include creating one table for each focus-group prompt or question, or for each evaluation question. Either way, this or some other kind of summary should appear in the analysis or reporting documentation to aid interpretation (and potentially be included in an appendix of the final evaluation report).

Interpreting Chinese Telecollaboration Results: Focusing on Evaluation Questions

When the data-analysis process has concluded, there should be a number of data summaries—of numerical and textual results—ready for evaluators to start the process of interpretation. Again, interpretation involves drawing conclusions about what the results mean in light of the evaluation questions. Interpretation, then, involves stepping back from the results, synthesizing the various sources of information, and trying to see the big-picture themes relevant to the project focus.

As noted a number of times, interpretation should focus closely on answering the evaluation questions. It is important that evaluators avoid straying from project foci or drawing conclusions irrelevant to users' and other stakeholders' concerns. Considering how to interpret the Chinese telecollaboration analyses in light of the evaluation questions, some questionnaire items and focus-group prompts clearly supply information relevant to a particular question. For example, for question 1 (on student satisfaction with the program), the relevant questionnaire items would appear to be the agreement-rating items on technology and course experiences, as well as the item asking students to rate their overall level of satisfaction with the course. In addition, the focus group prompt asking whether talking with language partners motivated students to continue studying

Table 9.4 Example summary of main themes from focus-group responses

Code	n	% of all codes	Example comments
Satisfied with program overall	7	16.3	I think the course was great. I got a lot of it. I really learned a lot of Chinese.
Effective – Authentic listening practice	6	14.0	It's pretty clear when what I've said isn't understood. So I have to try again and maybe say it a different way. Or maybe I have to figure out if it's my pronunciation or something. It's good. The pressure's on to be understood.
Effective – Learning from classmates	5	11.6	The discussion kind of helped. I learned how to say things from classmates that I would use sometimes during the chat. That helped me relax a bit before we started.
Effective – Plan to continue Chinese studies	5	11.6	I think there's a good chance. Maybe in a regular language class with more grammar and taking a Skype class as well. I think they'd work well together.
Effective – Interaction	4	9.3	Well what I like best is that it's real communication with a real speaker of the language and it's pretty clear when what I've said isn't understood. So I have to try again and maybe say it a different way. Or maybe I have to figure out if it's my pronunciation or something. It's good. The pressure's on to be understood.
Effective – Book topics prompts	4	9.3	I guess but my partner was kind of shy so it gave us something to talk about.
Noneffective – English during telecollaboration	4	9.3	When we had to speak English it got a little boring. I know they need to practice too, but it was still a little uninteresting.
Effective – Authentic speech	3	7.0	Yeah I liked that aspect too. Even though I hear a lot of Chinese at home I liked hearing the different accents and how people my age from Shanghai talk.
Unsatisfied – Unreliable technology	3	7.0	I lost the connection with my partner a lot. That was frustrating.
Noneffective – Book topics prompts	2	4.7	Sometimes the book was a little boring and it wasn't a great thing to talk about. The conversation kind of dragged sometimes. It was nicer when we could just talk about what we wanted.
Total	47	100.0	

Chinese might also supply evidence relevant to question 1. For question 2 (on effectiveness for student learning), the most relevant questionnaire information would seem to come from (1) the rating items asking about the usefulness of various course elements, (2) the overall course-usefulness item, and (3) the self-rated "can-do" statements indicating the extent to which students feel they have attained the course learning outcomes (and, by implication, indicating the effectiveness of the telecollaboration program). In addition, the focus-group prompt asking what students liked most about talking with their Chinese language partners also seems to provide information about what was effective for student language learning.

After identifying which results best match each evaluation question, it can be helpful to group and display the various summary tables and figures together in a single document or spreadsheet—organized by evaluation question. That way, the different sources of related results can be reviewed holistically for any findings emerging from the numerical and textual information taken together. For example, figure 9.3 and table 9.4 (and others) might be grouped together in a Word document to get a holistic sense of program effectiveness. What seems to be useful for language learning in general terms? Something in particular to look out for is where different types of results from different sources seem to reinforce each other. For example, a tentative conclusion that could be drawn in the telecollaboration scenario is that the technology-mediated interaction with the Chinese language partner during the program seems to be fairly effective for language learning—since it was rated highly for program usefulness on the questionnaire—and that the authentic interaction, in particular, provided valuable opportunities for developing language ability, particularly student listening skills (information gleaned from the focus-group data). Interpreting in this direction further, the evaluator might look to the student self-assessment items, other assessment results, and instructor interview results (among other sources of evidence) to get a sense of whether this conclusion holds across other sources of evidence as well. Again, the important takeaway is that interpretation and drawing conclusions from the various sets of results should be a disciplined activity always focused on answering the project evaluation questions.

Enhancing Evaluation Usefulness during Interpretation

The interpretation stage of the evaluation is especially prone to nonusefulness since it is a fundamentally subjective process. Different people can see different patterns and draw different conclusions from the same set of results. In addition, when conclusions drawn by one person do not correspond well to what others think are notable patterns in the results—particularly stakeholders—the trustworthiness of findings is undermined. Again, results, findings, and conclusions need to be regarded as accurate and legitimate by users in order for evaluation to be useful. All the careful evaluation planning and implementation laid out in this book comes to nothing if users have no confidence in the evaluation results or disagree with conclusions.

To avoid this outcome, we recommend that evaluators *collaboratively* interpret findings with evaluation users, or, if these individuals are unavailable, at least with other stakeholders or evaluation team members. Involving users in data interpretation, however, is the ideal scenario. Involving users helps them to come to their own conclusions about what the results mean, which is an effective way to avoid disagreements about findings and to provide users with directly relevant evaluation information. To this end, evaluators can organize "findings workshops" where results are summarized (using parsimonious data visualization) and presented to users to collaboratively review and draw conclusions. The role of the evaluator in this process is to facilitate the discussion, answer questions about data collection, and provide additional information or explanation along the way to aid the understanding and interpretation of the evaluation results.

In addition, once a set of conclusions has been established, a follow-up session can be scheduled to have users collaboratively generate recommendations and lay out a plan—with a timeline of key tasks and responsible individuals—mapping how the evaluation results will be used and by whom.

Of course, it may be that busy users will not be available for a series of meetings of this kind. If so, evaluators should try to either collaboratively interpret the results with a fellow evaluation team member, or, if working alone, have a colleague check their interpretations and conclusions.[6]

Notes

1. For experienced Excel users, the use of Excel "pivot tables" provides a much quicker analysis, though the discussion of more advanced Excel techniques goes beyond the scope of this volume.
2. Data visualization is now a professional subspecialization in the evaluation field. Two authors to consult on visualizing and presenting evaluation data effectively are Stephanie Evergreen (http://stephanieevergreen.com/) and Ann K. Emery (http://annkemery.com/).
3. The "find and replace" Excel feature can be used for this purpose.
4. Software packages such as NVivo, ATLAS.ti, MAXQDA, and others offer a number of useful features and affordances for analyzing textual and comments data. Licenses for these packages, however, are relatively expensive to purchase.
5. The approach we are proposing is a version of "content analysis," "a long and well-developed tradition ... where the issue is one of counting the frequency and sequencing of particular words, phrases, or concepts found in the data" (Miles, Huberman, and Saldaña 2014, 43).
6. For more detailed advice on data analysis numerical results see Brown (2001). For further information on qualitative data analysis see Miles, Huberman, and Saldaña (2014), and Saldaña (2016). For further reading on data visualization, see Evergreen (2017a, 2017b).

10

Key Points to Remember for Useful Evaluation

JOHN McE. DAVIS

WE CONCLUDE WITH A summary of the main points of the book. Below we list the key take-aways and high-priority practices to keep in mind when conducting evaluation in language programs with the aim of making the project as useful as possible for program stakeholders. The following points can be used as a checklist and referred to throughout the evaluation project to ensure best practices are being observed (referring to more detailed information available in the preceding chapters as needed).

Include Stakeholders throughout the Evaluation (Chapter 2)
Stakeholders must be involved at all stages of the evaluation project. Involvement of teachers, students, administrators, alumni, parents, and others during evaluation planning helps to make the evaluation respond to program stakeholders' needs and interests. Stakeholder involvement during data collection and interpretation helps stakeholders learn about their program and increases their ability to understand and use the evaluation results. Ultimately, stakeholder involvement and participation lead to greater evaluation ownership, which increases the likelihood of evaluation use and usefulness.

Undertake a Feasible Evaluation Project (Chapter 2)
Evaluation projects that try to collect too much data or take too long to complete run the risk of being conducted superficially or not finishing at all. Rushed or superficial evaluation will lack trustworthiness in the eyes of users and stakeholders. Evaluation that takes too long will fail to provide information in time for decision-making. Evaluation that fails to conclude is by definition nonuseful. During evaluation planning, then, make sure there are sufficient resources, personnel, and time to conduct the evaluation successfully.

Identify the Intended Users of the Evaluation (Chapter 3)

Ensure that there are clearly identified users of the evaluation project. Usually these will be decision-makers who have the power (and desire and interest) to take action on the basis of findings. Bring these people into the project early and involve them very closely in project planning. Make sure they understand their role in the evaluation—to be involved in key project decisions. Communicate with users throughout the project on important evaluation activities and milestones. Make sure users approve important project-planning elements, such as decisions about indicators, data-collection tools, strategies for reporting, and so on.

Identify Evaluation Uses (Chapter 3)

Do not assume what program decision-makers will use the evaluation for. Be explicit about what particular users will do with the evaluation results, and identify evaluation uses in consultation with project users. Head off anything that will threaten evaluation use. Take steps throughout the evaluation project to help ensure decision-makers can use the evaluation findings in the ways they want.

Formulate Evaluation Question(s) (Chapter 3)

Be explicit about what the evaluation project will investigate. The evaluation must have a clearly identified focus. Make sure the focus is expressed in one or more evaluation questions. Develop the questions in consultation with users and stakeholders (or stakeholder groups). Make sure the questions are clear, specific, answerable, researchable, and politically nonthreatening, and that they address a program feature that stakeholders care about.

Identify Indicators before Selecting Data-Collection Tools (Chapter 4)

Before deciding how to collect information, decide what type of information needs to be collected. List out the indicators of the relevant program processes that will help answer the evaluation questions. Make sure that users review and approve the indicators. Follow best practices to develop high-quality, useful indicators.

Use Indicators to Guide Selection of Evaluation Tools (Chapter 5)

Pay special attention to indicators when developing or selecting data-collection tools. Make sure that questionnaires, focus-group and interview protocols, assessments, and other tools capture all project indicators. If a data-collection instrument (or a part of the instrument) fails to collect information on a relevant project indicator, exclude it.

Ensure Users Approve Data-Collection Methods (Chapters 5)

Make sure that users get the information they want by having them review and approve the proposed data-collection methods. Make sure users are aware of the varieties of information and data that will be collected during the project and presented in the report (e.g., comments data or statistics), and check that users regard the information to come from the evaluation as relevant to their evaluation uses and decision-making needs.

Ensure Data Collection, Analysis, and Interpretation Lead to Trustworthy Findings (Chapter 9)

Evaluation usefulness will depend on users and stakeholders believing the evaluation findings and regarding the data-collection methods, analyses, and interpretations as trustworthy. Use best practices for developing and implementing data-collection tools. Take steps to ensure that data-collection strategies avoid bias and that they faithfully and reliably capture what they claim to capture. To the extent possible, involve stakeholders in data interpretation. Create opportunities for users and stakeholders to come to their own conclusions about findings and make recommendations.

Communicate with Stakeholders and Other Audiences throughout the Evaluation (Chapter 2)

Keep interested parties—particularly leadership and decision-makers—aware of evaluation activities and notable events using different channels of communication (email, social media, a project website, a project newsletter, periodic presentations, etc.). Circulate the project plan to stakeholders and other audiences, make data-collection tools available, make announcements about important project milestones, and report the findings using a variety of communication tools.

While the above points are all important for successful evaluation, what really makes evaluation consistently and meaningfully useful is a program-total effort where everyone in the program works energetically to help collect information and use evidence toward better understanding and improving educational effectiveness. Evaluation works best when it is something that educators value and endeavor to do well in the same way they value teacher development and training, curriculum and materials design, student assessment, budgeting, and so on. Put another way, evaluation makes an impact when it is integral to educational decision-making and has a "seat at the table" of program management. Of course, this type of systemic, evidence-based practice will require a sea change in mentality and program culture, but it is nevertheless an aim worth striving for, as evidenced by numerous language educators who have taken ownership of evaluation to useful effect in their programs. To aid readers in implementing evidence-based practice, this guide has endeavored to show high-quality practices that can help make evaluation a success in a language program and realize evaluation's potential for improving and enhancing language teaching and learning.

11

Example Evaluation Plan

TODD H. McKAY

WITH SO MANY MOVING parts in a program evaluation project, it is possible to lose sight of how everything fits together. A challenge for the evaluation team is ensuring that the various components of the evaluation project work together in a coherent way, data collection and analysis are carried out in a timely fashion, regular input and feedback are solicited from end-users and other program stakeholders, sufficient resources are allocated to sustain evaluation work, commitment to using findings is cultivated, and areas for ongoing and subsequent evaluation work are recorded. One way to capture the complexity of the evaluation process—and also to continue fostering engagement with the evaluation and use of findings—is to create an "evaluation plan." In this final chapter, we describe a prototypical evaluation plan and provide an example plan for the community college language lab scenario.

What is an Evaluation Plan?

An evaluation plan, as the name suggests, is a blueprint of the entire evaluation process. However, its function is more than simply providing written documentation of the evaluation work to be done. On the one hand, the evaluation plan is an organizational tool for the evaluator or project team, providing a summary of what is being evaluated, when actions are carried out, how implementation of the evaluation will proceed, and who will be directly or indirectly involved. On the other hand, the evaluation plan can also be used to foster evaluation use. That is, the evaluation plan should be a strategic tool to engage users in better understanding the evaluation, cultivating commitment to the evaluation, and promoting transparent evaluation practices. We have noted repeatedly that user and stakeholder involvement during evaluation planning is crucially important for evaluation usefulness. An evaluation plan should be the product of multiple negotiations and meetings with relevant decision-makers and a record of the various planning decisions that stakeholders, users, and the evaluator or evaluation team have made together. In addition, the final evaluation plan report must be submitted to evaluation users for their approval and circulated among stakeholders so that they are aware of what the project aims to accomplish and how it has been designed with their interests in mind. At the end of the evaluation, when the final report is submitted, there should be no methodological surprises. The evaluation plan, then, is an opportunity to ensure that everyone approves the next steps. Furthermore, the evaluation team might consider creative ways of communicating the plan to users and stakeholders. In addition to simply emailing the report to relevant individuals, a user meeting or public presentation are possible options. The important point is that the creation and circulation of the evaluation plan is an opportunity to generate user buy-in and modify any aspects of the project that users dislike that may thereby hinder evaluation usefulness.

Structure of an Evaluation Plan

An evaluation plan conventionally consists of some combination of the following components:

1. Introduction and program description
2. List of stakeholders and stakeholder engagement plan
3. Users and uses
4. Evaluation or project questions
5. Indicators and information sources
6. Analysis and interpretation
7. Plan for disseminating and using evaluation findings
8. Timeline

While many of these components have been discussed individually in previous chapters, some are newly introduced here, such as the stakeholder engagement plan, steps for analysis and interpretation, and the plan for disseminating and using findings. The example evaluation plan below illustrates one way in which evaluation project components can be brought together to guide evaluation work. How the evaluation plan takes shape and is carried out, of course, depends on evaluation users, the questions being asked, and the context in which the evaluation unfolds. The following is a template that can (and should) be modified and adapted to readers' educational contexts.

Maguire Community College Language Media Lab: Evaluation Plan

In recent years, there has been a rapid expansion and proliferation of educational technologies for language-learning purposes, with implications for how language students and teachers use language centers at colleges and universities. In light of these trends, instructors at the Maguire Community College (MCC) Language Media Lab (LML), with the support of the chair of the Department of Humanities, are conducting an evaluation of the LML over the spring and summer 2018 semesters to investigate the usefulness of the lab for various stakeholders.

Evaluation Purpose

The evaluation aims to better understand the relevance of the LML in light of local stakeholder needs and recent trends in educational technology and contemporary uses of language labs at US community colleges (CCs). The main goal of the project is to identify ways in which the LML can best support MCC students and faculty in the teaching and learning of foreign languages.

Stakeholders
The following individuals and groups are identified as stakeholders in the MCC LML evaluation project:

- Dr. Camila Torres, Dean, Division of Liberal Arts, MCC
- Dr. Supriti Sarkar, Director, Center for Teaching and Learning Excellence, MCC
- Dr. Mary Watson, Director of English Language Center, MCC
- Elena Cooper, Coordinator, Hill Valley CC Language Media Center
- Robert Nunez, Coordinator, Harrison CC Language and Technology Center
- MCC Language Instructors
- MCC Student Council

The above individuals and groups will be involved in evaluation activities and receive communications about the LML evaluation project as shown in Table 1.

Users
The following individuals are identified as the primary intended users of the evaluation:

- Dr. Lifen Han, Chair, Department of Humanities
- Wataru Tanaka, LML coordinator

Project Uses
Dr. Lifen Han and Wataru Tanaka have committed to using the evaluation project for the following programmatic actions and decisions:

1. Better understand how well the lab supports the language-learning needs of LML users
2. Identify the range of needs, uses, and users the LML does not support currently
3. Identify needed improvements and changes given current and future needs of LML users
4. Demonstrate the value of technology-mediated language learning to the campus community

Project Team
Five MCC staff compose the evaluation project team:

- Soim Choi, Full-time Korean instructor
- Wataru Tanaka, LML coordinator
- Dr. Farhana Khan, Adjunct professor of Urdu
- Sean O'Connor, Full-time ESL instructor
- Yusuf Goren, MCC student, LML lab assistant

Soim Choi is leading the project team and has received a six-credit course reduction to facilitate the evaluation in spring and summer of 2018.

Evaluation Questions
The project is guided by two evaluation questions:

1. How well is the lab currently supporting language education at the college?
2. What changes or innovations are needed to better support lab users and campus stakeholders?

Indicators, Methods, Informants, Sources
Table 2 shows how information will be collected to shed light on both evaluation questions.

Analysis and Interpretation Plan
Soim Choi will be the primary individual responsible for analyzing data. Soim will provide descriptive statistics and response counts for questionnaire data and will code interview transcriptions and identify themes using an emergent-themes approach in NVivo.

All results will be analyzed and summarized and made available to evaluation users for an interpretation workshop/meeting. The evaluation team will facilitate an interpretation session with Dr. Lifen Han to draw conclusions from project results. User interpretations will be summarized into an executive findings summary (two pages) and submitted to Dr. Camila Torres, Dr. Lifen Han, Dr. Supriti Sarkar, Dr. Mary Watson, Elena Cooper, and Robert Nunez.

Dissemination and Use Plan
The evaluation team will write a final report using the findings from the interpretation workshop and executive summary. The report will be submitted to Dr. Lifen Han and all project stakeholders. The report will be publicly available via the project SharePoint site.

Main findings from the report will be presented at a public presentation. Immediately following the presentation, the project team and users will convene to collaboratively generate recommendations and plan for use of the evaluation findings. A timeline of events and responsible parties will be generated to plan for evaluation use.

Members of the evaluation team will also continue to meet on a biweekly basis to identify how the LML can continue to better meet the needs of the FL community. Table 3 sets out a time line of events for key evaluation activities.

• Table 1 Stakeholder engagement plan

Stakeholder	Engagement strategy						
	Kick-off meeting	Project plan presentation	Project plan	Email newsletter	SharePoint site	Final report	Report presentation
Dr. Camila Torres	✓	⋯	✓	✓	⋯	✓	⋯
Dr. Supriti Sarkar	✓	✓	✓	✓	✓	✓	✓
Dr. Mary Watson	✓	✓	✓	✓	✓	✓	✓
Elena Cooper	✓	✓	✓	✓	✓	✓	✓
Robert Nunez	✓	✓	✓	✓	✓	✓	✓
MCC Language Instructors	⋯	⋯	⋯	✓	✓	✓	✓
MCC Student Council	⋯	⋯	⋯	✓	⋯	✓	✓

● Table 2 Evaluation questions, methods, informants, sources

Evaluation question	Indicator	Method	Informant/Source
How well is the language lab supporting language education at the college?	1. Number/Frequency of lab visitors	Document analysis	Lab records
	2. Type of lab visitor	Questionnaire	MCC faculty
			MCC students
	3. Most and least frequent uses of the language lab by visitors and staff	Questionnaire	MCC faculty
			MCC students
		Interview	LML staff
			MCC faculty
	4. Most and least frequently used lab equipment or technology	Questionnaire	MCC faculty
			MCC students
		Interview	LML staff
			MCC faculty
	5. Use of lab space by lab visitors	Questionnaire	MCC faculty
			MCC students
		Interview	LML staff
			MCC faculty
	6. Usefulness of current lab resources, equipment or technology, and spaces for campus stakeholders	Questionnaire	MCC faculty
			MCC students
		Interview	LML staff
			MCC faculty
	7. Satisfaction with lab resources, equipment or technology, and spaces by campus stakeholders	Questionnaire	MCC faculty
			MCC students
		Interview	LML staff
			MCC faculty
	8. Deterrents to lab use or visitation	Focus group	MCC faculty
			MCC students
		Interview	LML staff
			MCC faculty

(continued)

Evaluation question	Indicator	Method	Informant/Source
What changes or innovations are needed to better support lab users and campus stakeholders?	1. Desired uses of the language lab by users, staff, and campus stakeholders	Questionnaire Interview	MCC faculty MCC students LML staff MCC faculty Administrators
	2. Desired lab equipment or technology by users, staff, and campus stakeholders	Questionnaire Interview	MCC faculty MCC students LML staff MCC faculty Administrators
	3. Desired spaces by users, staff, and campus stakeholders	Questionnaire Interview	MCC faculty MCC students LML staff MCC faculty Administrators
	4. Best practices in college language labs and media centers at peer institutions	Interview	Lab directors at peer institutions
	5. Best practices in media-center activities, innovation, and support at US colleges and universities	Document analysis /literature review	Published research studies

Table 3 Timeline of events

Action	When	Who
Collect logbook information on visitor lab use	Early January	Wataru Tanaka
Conduct interviews with LML staff[1]	Mid–late January	Soim Choi
		Sean O'Connor
Transcribe LML staff interviews	Early February	Yusuf Goren
Analyze/Code LML staff interviews	Mid February	Soim Choi
Provide item list for electronic questionnaire	Mid February	Soim Choi
Design electronic questionnaire	Late February	Wataru Tanaka
Pilot electronic questionnaire with project team	Late February	Wataru Tanaka
Revise and administer questionnaire to FL students, faculty, and staff	Late February	Wataru Tanaka
Analyze questionnaire data	Early March	Soim Choi
Conduct interviews (5–10) with FL faculty and administrators[2]	March	Soim Choi
		Sean O'Connor
		Dr. Farhana Khan
Analyze/Code FL faculty and administrator interviews	Early April	Soim Choi
Analyze scholarly research on "best practices"	April	Soim Choi
Schedule interpretation/workshop meetings with project team and users	Early May	Soim Choi
		Dr. Lifen Han
		Wataru Tanaka
		Dr. Farhana Khan
		Sean O'Connor
		Yusuf Goren
Summarize discussion from interpretation/workshop meeting into two-page executive summary	Mid May	Soim Choi
Circulate executive summary to stakeholder group	Mid May	Soim Choi
Draft detailed final report	Late May	Soim Choi
Group revisions to final report	Late May	Soim Choi
Submit final report to user and stakeholder groups	Early June	Soim Choi
Make report available (with login) via project SharePoint site	Early June	Soim Choi
Schedule public presentation to share findings and follow-up meeting to plan for findings use	Early June	Soim Choi
		Attendees

(continued)

Action	When	Who
Generate timeline of events/actions (along with responsible parties) for using findings	Early June	Soim Choi Dr. Lifen Han Wataru Tanaka Dr. Farhana Khan Sean O'Connor Yusuf Goren
Plan and schedule regular, biweekly meetings to facilitate concrete changes at LML	Mid June–August	Soim Choi Dr. Lifen Han Wataru Tanaka Dr. Farhana Khan Sean O'Connor Yusuf Goren

1. Wataru Tanaka will not conduct interviews with LML staff, given his position as coordinator.

2. Dr. Khan will not conduct interviews with faculty in similar positions, nor with adjunct or part-time faculty.

References

Bader, Gloria E., and Catherine A. Rossi. 2002. *Focus Groups: A Step-by-Step Guide.* San Diego: The Bader Group.

Brown, James Dean. 2001. *Using Surveys in Language Programs.* Cambridge: Cambridge University Press.

Bryson, John M., Michael Quinn Patton, and Ruth A. Bowman. 2011. "Working with Evaluation Stakeholders: A Rationale, Step-Wise Approach and Toolkit." *Evaluation and Program Planning* 34:1–12.

Colker, Alexis Mitman. N.d. "Developing Interviews: Preparing an Interview Protocol." Online Evaluation Resource Library. http://oerl.sri.com/module/mod6/m6_p1.html.

Davis, John McE. 2011. *Using Surveys for Understanding and Improving Foreign Language Programs.* Foreign Language Program Evaluation Project. Honolulu: University of Hawaiʻi, National Foreign Language Resource Center. http://hdl.handle.net/10125/14549.

———. 2015. "Sampling and What It Means." In *The Cambridge Guide to Research in Language Teaching and Learning,* edited by James Dean Brown and Christine Coombe, 198–205. Cambridge: Cambridge University Press.

Dillman, Don A. 2000. *Mail and Internet Surveys: The Tailored Design Method.* New York: John Wiley and Sons.

Dillman, Don A., Jolene D. Smyth, and Leah Melani Christian. 2014. *Internet, Mail, and Mixed-Mode Surveys: The Tailored Design Method.* 3rd ed. Hoboken, NJ: John Wiley and Sons.

Dörnyei, Zoltán, and Tatsuya Taguchi. 2010. *Questionnaires in Second Language Research: Construction, Administration, and Processing.* 2nd ed. New York: Routledge.

Evergreen, Stephanie D. H. 2017a. *Effective Data Visualization: The Right Chart for the Right Data.* Los Angeles: Sage.

———. 2017b. *Presenting Data Effectively: Communicating Your Findings for Maximum Impact.* Los Angeles: Sage.

Fern, Edward F. 2001. *Advanced Focus Group Research.* Thousand Oaks, CA: Sage.

Grudens-Schuck, Nancy, Beverlyn Lundy Allen, and Kathlene Larson. 2004. "Methodology Brief: Focus Group Fundamentals." *Extension Community and Economic Development Publications.* http://lib.dr.iastate.edu/cgi/viewcontent.cgi?article=1011&context=extension_communities_pubs.

Iarossi, Giuseppe. 2006. *The Power of Survey Design: A User's Guide for Managing Surveys, Interpreting Results, and Influencing Respondents.* Washington, DC: The World Bank.

Johnson, Kelli, Lija O. Greenseid, Stacie A. Toal, Jean A. King, Frances Lawrenz, and Boris Volkov. 2009. "Research on Evaluation Use: A Review of the Empirical Literature from 1986 to 2005." *American Journal of Evaluation* 30:377–410.

Krueger, Richard A., and Mary Anne Casey. 2009. *Focus Groups: A Practical Guide for Applied Research.* 4th ed. Thousand Oaks, CA: Sage.

Kvale, Steinar. 1996. *InterViews: An Introduction to Qualitative Research Interviewing.* Thousand Oaks, CA: Sage.

Larson, Kathlene, Nancy Grudens-Schuck, and Beverlyn Lundy Allen. 2004. "Can You Call It a Focus Group?" *Methodology Brief.* Iowa State University Extension. https://store.extension.iastate.edu/Product/pm1969a-pdf.

Lennie, June, Jo Tacchi, Bikash Koirala, Michael Wilmore, and Andrew Skuse. 2011. "Equal Access Participatory Monitoring and Evaluation Toolkit: Setting Objectives and Indicators." http://www.betterevaluation.org/sites/default/files/EA_PM%26E_toolkit_module_2_objectives%26indicators_for_publication.pdf.

Lynch, Brian K. 2000. "Evaluating a Project-Oriented CALL Innovation." *Computer Assisted Language Learning* 13:417–40.

Marczak, Mary, and Meg Sewell. 1991. "Using Focus Groups for Evaluation." University of Arizona. https://cals.arizona.edu/sfcs/cyfernet/cyfar/focus.htm.

Mendelow, A. L. 1981. "Environmental Scanning—The Impact of the Stakeholder Concept." In International Conference on Information Systems (ICIS) 1981 Proceedings, 407–18. http://aisel.aisnet.org/cgi/viewcontent.cgi?article=1009&context=icis1981.

Miles, Matthew B., A. Michael Huberman, and Johnny Saldaña. 2014. *Qualitative Data Analysis: A Methods Sourcebook.* Thousand Oaks, CA: Sage.

Norris, John M. 2006. "The Why (and How) of Assessing Student Learning Outcomes in College Foreign Language Programs." *Modern Language Journal* 90 (4): 576–83. doi:10.1111/j.1540-4781.2006.00466_2.x.

———. 2008. *Validity Evaluation in Language Assessment.* New York: Peter Lang.

———. 2016. "Language Program Evaluation." *Modern Language Journal* 100:169–89. doi:10.1111/modl.12307.

Norris, John M., and John McEwan Davis. 2015. *Student Learning Outcomes Assessment in College Foreign Language Programs.* Honolulu: University of Hawai'i, National Foreign Language Resource Center.

Norris, John M., John McEwan Davis, Castle Sinicrope, and Yukiko Watanabe. 2009. *Toward Useful Program Evaluation in College Foreign Language Education.* Honolulu: National Foreign Language Resource Center.

Oppenheim, Abraham Naftali. 1992. *Questionnaire Design, Interviewing, and Attitude Measurement.* London: Pinter.

Patten, Mildred L. 2001. *Questionnaire Research: A Practical Guide.* Los Angeles: Pyrczak.

Patton, Michael Quinn. 1990. *Qualitative Evaluation and Research Methods.* Thousand Oaks, CA: Sage.

———. 2008. *Utilization-Focused Evaluation.* Thousand Oaks, CA: Sage.

———. 2015. *Qualitative Research and Evaluation Methods.* Thousand Oaks, CA: Sage.

Saldaña, Johnny. 2016. *The Coding Manual for Qualitative Researchers.* Thousand Oaks, CA: Sage.

Warwick, Donald P., and Charles Andrew Lininger. 1975. *The Sample Survey: Theory and Practice.* New York: McGraw Hill.

Wiggins, Grant P., and Jay McTighe. 2005. *Understanding by Design.* 2nd ed. Alexandria, VA: Association for Supervision and Curriculum Development.

Yarbrough, Donald. B., Lyn M. Shulha, Rodney K. Hopson, and Flora A. Caruthers. 2011. *The Program Evaluation Standards: A Guide for Evaluators and Evaluation Users.* Thousand Oaks, CA: Sage.

Contributors

John McE. Davis is an evaluation specialist at the Foreign Service Institute, School of Language Studies, US Department of State (Yorktown Systems Group, Contractor). His research interests are in language assessment, pedagogy, and useful implementation of educational evaluation in language programs.

Todd H. McKay is a PhD candidate and research assistant for the Assessment and Evaluation Language Resource Center at Georgetown. His interests are program evaluation, task-based language teaching, statistics, and measurement. Todd is former director of the Bangla Critical Language Scholarship Program and Junior Fellow with American Institute of Bangladesh Studies.

Lara Bryfonski is a PhD candidate at Georgetown University. Her research focuses on interaction in second language acquisition, task-based language teaching, and language program evaluation. Lara has designed and conducted focus groups to evaluate programs with the US Foreign Service Institute and Georgetown University, as well as in her own research. Lara is a licensed English as a second language (ESL) teacher and has taught ESL in a variety of contexts in the United States and abroad.

Cristi Vallejos is a PhD candidate in Spanish Applied Linguistics at Georgetown University where she also serves as a Spanish instructor and research assistant. She has conducted research in language program evaluation, phonological acquisition in higher education, study abroad contexts, and second language writing.

Amy I. Kim is a PhD candidate in Applied Linguistics at Georgetown University, where she serves as a graduate student research assistant at the Assessment and Evaluation Language Resource Center. Her research draws on a range of qualitative and quantitative research methodologies, focusing on second and foreign language assessment, task-based language teaching, and program evaluation.

Jorge Méndez Seijas is a PhD candidate in the Spanish Applied Linguistics program at Georgetown University. Jorge has taught language courses and served as a course coordinator at Georgetown University and Princeton University. Jorge's research interests include second language phonology, heritage language education, and language program evaluation.

Francesca Venezia is a PhD candidate in Applied Linguistics at Georgetown University and has worked as a research assistant for the Assessment and Evaluation Language Resource Center. Her research interests include heritage language education, program evaluation, and language pedagogy. She has experience teaching English and Spanish in various settings.

Janire Zalbidea is a PhD candidate in Spanish Applied Linguistics at Georgetown University, where she has also taught courses on linguistics and teacher education and served as assistant director for the Intensive Basic and Intermediate Spanish programs. Her research focuses primarily on instructed second language acquisition and technology-enhanced task-based language teaching.

CPSIA information can be obtained
at www.ICGtesting.com
Printed in the USA
BVOW08s1436050118
504536BV00001B/4/P